MW01205347

Write Your Own Palm® Software!

Developing your own applications using the
ACCESS™ Garnet® OS Development Suite

Charles Tatum II

I have a lot of people to whom I want to dedicate this book, my first:

To my family – my mother and brother Robert, and my late father – thanks for your support.

And to the many wonderful people I've met in Houston particularly:

Sean M., a long-time friend on whom I can always count on for great conversation, thank you.

David F., a good friend and supporter, thanks for being there.

Robbie H., a great guy who's peppy and positive, and who's going places.

Charlie S., a friendly, smiling face I'd want to see after a long trip.

Randy W., a fellow geek.

Omar, 'cuz you're so crazy!

Marcus C. & Vanessa V., Travis & Tiffany – the CAM is much more fun with you guys.

Jackie D. & Pam G. – I've shared more laughs with you two than I can remember, thank you so much!

Bucky T., because to know him is to love him. Who doesn't love Bucky?

Marshall F., a smart guy who's going places in the hotel industry!

The "Hollywood" bunch: Rupert, Mark F., Merlyn & Scott C., Mark S.; James, Ryan, Mark, Seth and Wei behind the counter; T.J. & Blair, Ryan T. & Jesse, and all the rest – thanks for making my nights and weekends.

David S. and Patrick A. – two of my favorite ex-baristas, always entertaining … and unpredictable.

The gang at all my haunts – Antidote, Inversion Coffee, Waldo's and Starbucks Midtown – you keep me on an even keel.

Jonathan O., who's working on a book of his own.

The communities of Montrose, The Heights and the Museum District – the *real* Houston!

And to my friends in Austin – especially Alex, Hans, Chris, Lee and Tyler – thanks for the fun times at the house.

Wayne M., a deep thinker and supportive friend with whom I enjoy exchanging e-mails and talking about life.

Scott, Jack, Travis, Richard and the other good folks at Mangia Pizza.

And, finally, a big word of thanks to my alma mater, The University Of Illinois at Urbana-Champaign, one of the best computer science institutions in the country, for providing me a great foundation on which to build my career in the field of information technology. To each and every Illini student and alumnus, I salute you all. GO ILLINI!

Contents

1. Introduction

What This Book Is

This book is for those interested in writing their own Palm® software, for themselves and for those with whom they want to share. Its key audience is hobbyist programmers, particularly those with an interest in writing shareware applications. Shareware applications, if you don't happen to know, is a sort of cottage business (I hesitate to call it an industry) where the applications are distributed freely and then customers, if they like the software, send a registration fee to the developer(s).

This book is also an attempt at a structured course in Palm development. I begin with very simple exercises to build your confidence and, as you master simpler programs, ratchet up the difficulty level. You may stop at any time when you have as much as you wish; you do not have to go all the way through all the chapters if you have found what you want.

You may also note that I have included certain commentary directed at Microsoft Visual Basic® developers. That is because I am one myself, and felt that something to tie the worlds of Visual Basic and C together would make it easier for those individuals to get Palm C, thus making it more accessible. If the Visual Basic comments don't apply to you, please feel free to skip them.

What This Book Is Not

This is not intended to be a book on how to program. You already need to have some know-how in the basics of computer programming and writing software, even on a basic level, before jumping in. (In other words, if you don't know the difference between a do-loop and an onion ring you're already in over your head.) I'm going to assume if you're reading this, that you already know about basic concepts such as looping and other control structures, data types, assignment statements, calling subroutines, creating functions, and coordinate systems on a screen (x,y point system).

You'd be better off starting with a low-level programming course (preferably in C or C++) before sitting down to this. I do have a crash-course on the C language in this book, but it is for experienced programmers (especially Visual Basic programmers of which I am one) seeking to make a transition over (Visual Basic is a much more user-friendly language, is easier to write, and is a harder language in which to make mistakes).

This is also not a book intended for use by, let's just say, "corporate" types – high-powered programmers who are looking to write Palm solutions for organizations or enterprises. Most such companies usually have more acute time constraints and would not have the patience to work through most of what's contained herein. In addition, they would probably have their developers using pre-fabricated development environments.

Finally, and possibly the biggest disappointment for some of you, this book DOES NOT cover ACCESS Company's new ACCESS Linux Platform Development System. To begin with, that environment has not been out for long (it wasn't that old when this book went to press) and there aren't any devices that use it. The Garnet® platform, on the other hand, is being used by literally millions of Palm devices including Palm's newest offering, the Centro™.

Believe me, Garnet isn't going anywhere anytime soon.

Prerequisites

Before you continue I suggest you have all the following in your arsenal:

- One year or more experience writing software in a programming language (C, C++, Visual Basic)

- A Palm device of your own such as a Centro™, T|X™, or Treo™ smartphone

- A desktop or notebook computer running Windows Vista®, Windows XP® (SP 2+) or Windows 2000® (SP 4) at 800 MHz or faster, with 2 GB hard drive space free for installing the Garnet OS Development Suite as well as workspace for the projects you'll be building

- A **lot** of patience

I cannot underemphasize the importance of that last item, **patience**. You will find that writing for the Palm environment, even if you're a seasoned programmer like me, will try your patience at times. I have sat down to write a project in what I thought would take "X" amount of time, and it wound up taking 3X (three times) that.

Why Program For The Palm?

So why write software for the Palm in this era in which Apple's iPhone™ is hip, and in which Windows Mobile has its own loyal followers? There are several good reasons.

Free Development Tools. First of all, the Palm development tools from ACCESS are free of charge. For you to write in Windows Mobile® using the Visual Studio® platform you'd have to shell out quite a bit. (The folks at Microsoft didn't think to make it possible to generate executable code using Visual Basic .NET® which runs only $129. Trust me, I bought it and found this out the hard way.)

Millions of Palm users. At the time of this writing, the Palm line included the Z22, the Tungsten E2, the T|X, the Treo, and the new Centro. This doesn't even include all the other Palm users out there clinging to their m-series PDA's, Handspring™ Visor™ and Visor Prism™ devices, Sony® Clie® devices and other such machines. Trust me, there are plenty of Palm users out there.

Royalty-Free Distribution, No Interpreters, Easy Sharing. When you generate a Palm application into its finished state with GDS, it doesn't require anything else to run it. In the past, "pseudo-code" interpreters from some companies were required to run Palm-generated applications created with their tools, but that interpreter had to be distributed with the programs, which used up additional space on the end users' devices.

With Apple's iPhone software development kit, Windows users are shut out (one must have a Mac workstation to use it as of the date of this writing), and to list the software at Apple's developer store web site costs at least $99.

Palm software has no such limitations. When you write an application for a Palm device, it will be in "native" code, meaning machine-level instructions will be interpreted directly by the Palm PDA's CPU. Once the program is complete and you're ready to share it with others or sell it, there are no royalties to pay back to Palm or ACCESS. And sharing is as easy as beaming a Palm application from your device to a friend's device!

Good Way To Learn C. I had never really had a good excuse for learning the C language until I decided to learn to write for the Palm platform. For years I've been a big fan of Visual Basic (which is why you'll hear me talk about it a lot throughout this book). I had avoided the C language for most of the reasons I'd heard – ugly source code, less forgiving compilers, etc.

Programming in C on the Palm lets you concentrate on, essentially, just a few input-output concepts – the controls, the screen, and a database (actually just a binary file; more on that later). No concerns about printers, networks, security, etc. I personally tend to learn most effectively in an environment that is simpler, and the Palm platform provides it.

Palm's Great User Interface. Palm doesn't have an icon for "please wait". (In Microsoft's world it's often the hourglass symbol.) Palm's menu system has simple icons, and to start a program, you only need tap an icon once. Similar to Windows, Palm programs have their own consistency in title bars, menu structures, buttons, fields, and fonts.

Caution: GDS Has Bugs

Having established that writing for the Palm environment is a worthwhile pursuit, I have to say that you may occasionally notice behavior that appears incorrect. You may code something expecting one behavior and you don't get that behavior. It may not necessarily be your program's logic. It may also be GDS: I have observed that it has bugs.

This is why patience is so important to the Palm programming process. If one technical approach to solving a problem doesn't work, you may need to find another one – one that takes twice as many lines to code, but reliably delivers the same result.

This book does not contain a bug list; just know that occasionally you may see a head-scratcher that you may spend hours on trying to debug, only to reach the conclusion that, yes, your coding is correct and that (for some reason) the compiled code is wrong. Best to just move on.

Using GDS On Vista

I mention the bug thing because having used GDS on Windows Vista (and its predecessor, Palm OS® Development Suite on Windows XP), I can say that there are still some irregularities I have learned to work around. The Garnet OS Development System is not, to my knowledge, certified for use on Windows

Vista. That, of course, doesn't mean you *can't* use it under Vista; you just may get some unexpected behaviors when compiling your software.

About Code Segments

Throughout this book, you will see code segments using `this font`. Some lines will wrap around from line to line, as in this example in the C language:

```
case pushButtonC:
    pField = FrmGetObjectPtr(pForm, FrmGetObjectIndex(pForm,
fldButtons));
```

or this example in the Visual Basic language:

```
            MessageBox.Show("You have fewer lines in your data file than the
number you specified.  Extra lines will be blank records.", "Short Data File",
MessageBoxButtons.OK, MessageBoxIcon.Exclamation)
```

Be sure to type lines that wrap to successive lines as **one long, continuous line** without pressing the **Enter** key to break the lines apart. You may need to read the line more carefully to check the context and ensure the line runs on. Failure to type longer lines correctly may produce syntax errors which will stop your program from running, or may result in unexpected program behavior.

2. A Crash Course In C

Okay… for those of you that are rusty at C, or have never used it, this chapter is for you. It is practically required reading. If you've never worked with C and you don't read this chapter, I'm not responsible for the hair loss you'll suffer from ripping it out in anguish.

I happen to be a big fan of Microsoft's Visual Basic language and found that learning C was a considerable challenge. So, for those of you who are (like I was at one time) unfamiliar with the C language, this chapter is to help you bridge between the two languages. In this chapter, I will point out some of the differences between "VB" and C. Do try to keep an open mind even though what you're about to see may be exotic and strange. Those of you who are C, C++ or C# veterans, you may skip this entire chapter; all you'll really need to learn in terms of coding will be Palm's API functions.

Ready?

Coding Conventions

Use semi-colons. Like PL/I, Pascal, and a host of other languages, C requires you to place a semi-colon after each statement. If you don't, when you compile the program you'll get what's called a "parse error", which is a syntax error. Here's a code segment showing what some typical C code looks like:

```
x = (Int16)penX;
y = (Int16)penY;
WinDisplayToWindowPt( &x, &y );

rect.topLeft.x = boardX + boardFrameMargin;
rect.topLeft.y = boardY + boardFrameMargin;
```

Okay, well, maybe that's not *typical*. That only looks dreadful now because you don't have the context. I assure you it actually does something useful.

Case sensitivity. C is a case-sensitive language, which means you'll have to be very careful not to redefine a variable just because you spell it differently. In C, all the following would be considered different variables:

```
Char FirstName[70];
Char firstname[70];
Char FIRSTNAME[70];
```

Whereas in Visual Basic, the compiler would say, in effect, "You already defined that, dummy."

Why does this matter? Well, if you've been poring over a program for hours because it didn't behave as you thought, this is one of those headslappers that could surprise you... you may simply have mistyped your variable name using the wrong case.

Comments. Any code you don't want to execute can be "commented out", meaning each line is preceded by a pair of forward slashes, like so:

```
// Load the form resource.  THIS IS A COMMENT.
formId = eventP->data.frmLoad.formID;
frmP = FrmInitForm(formId);
FrmSetActiveForm(frmP);
```

On the following pages are some helpful tables summarizing some of Palm C's different data types. These lists are not exhaustive; they're intended to present the functions and structures you'll likely use the most.

Numeric Data Types

Palm C Data Type	What It Is	Variable Declarations In Palm C	Equivalent Declarations In Visual Basic
Int8, Int16, Int32	Integers for 8-bit, 16-bit and 32-bit numbers, respectively. Long integers are 32 bits. What are the capacities of each number? Do the math. These can contain positive and negative numbers.	Int8 temp_chg; Int16 stock_price; Int32 iq_level;	Dim temp_chg as Integer Dim stock_price as Integer Dim iq_level as Long
UInt8, UInt16, UInt32	Unsigned integers for 8-bit, 16-bit and 32-bit numbers, respectively. Unsigned long integers are 32 bits. In other words, positive numbers only. Use these for things you count.	UInt8 shoesize; UInt16 channels; UInt32 population;	Dim shoesize as Integer Dim channels as Integer Dim population as Long
FlpCompDouble	Floating-point, double-precision numbers use this. But it's not as straightforward as it sounds. There are no single precision numbers – no usable ones, anyway. More on that later. Use these for any number with fractions, such as dollar amounts or bowling averages.	FlpCompDouble mySalary; FlpCompDouble myRaise; FlpCompDouble myBonus;	Dim mySalary as Double Dim myRaise as Double Dim myBonus as Double
Boolean	Boolean variable. Has values true and false. (Same as yes and no, on and off, maybe and maybe not.) Use these to keep track of whether something has been done or not, selected or not, finished or not, or to track whether something is or is not.	Boolean IsSmart; Boolean IsSexy; Boolean IsRich;	Dim IsSmart as Boolean Dim IsSexy as Boolean Dim IsRich as Boolean

Numeric Operations

Palm C Operator	What It Is	Use In C	Use In Visual Basic
=	Assignment, setting the value of a variable to what's on the right of the sign. NOTE: For Floating-point numbers it's a little different; more on that later.	x = 3;	x = 3
+, -, *, /	Addition, subtraction, multiplication, division	a = b + c; c = (f - 32) * (5/9);	a = b + c c = (f - 32) * (5/9)
++, --	Increment by 1, decrement by 1, commonly used in loop control.	n++ x--	No equivalent.
!	Boolean NOT. Changes a Boolean value to its opposite.	ready = !ready;	ready = Not ready

All the typical rules of using parentheses apply, just like anywhere else. Expressions are evaluated from innermost to outermost, then from left to right.

Everything else you want to do with numbers (such as floating-point, trigonometric operations) you have to use a MathLib *function*. See "MathLib Functions" in Chapter 15 for details.

Character Data Types

Palm C Data Type	What It Is	Variable Declarations In Palm C	Equivalent Declarations In Visual Basic

Character String (Array)	The same as a character string ... sort of. In C, if you have a string of 20 characters, what you really have is an array of 20 individual characters. And the first position in the array is numbered 0, not 1. See "Arrays", below.	`Char nickname[40];`
		`Char petname[60];`
		`Char secret[100];`
			`Dim nickname as`
			`String*40`
			`Dim petname as`
			`String*60`
			`Dim secret at`
			`String*100`

Character String (Pointer)	The same as a character array ... sort of. A character string represented with a pointer doesn't have to have a fixed length at its declaration. Sometimes you'll find this convenient, other times you'll hate it. DO NOT assume this is the same thing as a variable-length string, though, because it isn't.	`Char *drink;`
		`Char *flavor;`
		`Char *brand;`
			`Dim drink as String`
			`Dim flavor as String`
			`Dim brand as String`
			`(note the difference`
			`from the cell above)`

Single Character	Exactly what it sounds like, a character string of length 1.	`Char mathgrade;`
		`Char gymgrade;`
		`Char artgrade;`
			`Dim mathgrade as`
			`String*1`
			`Dim gymgrade as`
			`String*1`
			`Dim artgrade as`
			`String*1`

Character Operations

Palm C Operator	What It Is	Use In C	Use In Visual Basic

=	Assignment (pointer strings only)	`*clown = "Bozo";`
		`*character =`
		`"Whizzo";`
			`clown = "Bozo"`
			`character = "Whizzo"`

Basically, that's about all you can directly do with a character string. You'll be using Palm API functions for everything else:

Character Functions

Function	What It Is	Use In C	Use In Visual Basic
StrCopy(target,src)	Assign or copy the value of one string to another	`StrCopy(endpoint,` `startpoint);`	`endpoint =` `startpoint`
StrCat(target, app)	Append a string to follow a target string	`StrCat(base, newstr);`	`base = base &` `newstr`
StrIToA(str, int)	Change an integer into a character string.	`StrIToA(score_str,` `score);`	`score_str =` `CStr(score)`

StrAToI(str)	Change a string into an integer	`score =`
		`StrAToI(score_str);`
			`score =`
			`CInt(score_str)`
			`score =`
			`Val(score_str)`

Control Constructs

Construct	What It's For	Use In C	Use In Visual Basic
if/then	If a certain condition is true, do what's in the block of code.	```if (score > 90) { grade = 'A'; graduate = 'Y'; }```	```If score > 90 Then grade = "A" graduate = "Y" End If```
if/then/else	Same as if/then, except you explicitly define a block of code to execute if the condition fails.	```if (score > 60) { pass = 'Y'; } else { fail = 'Y'; }```	```If score > 60 Then pass = "Y" Else fail = "Y" End If```
for-loop (also known informally as a do-loop)	When you want to perform something a certain number of times	```for (n = 1; n <= 10; n++) { color[n] = 255; }```	```For n = 1 to 10 color(n) = 255 Next n```
do-while loop	When you want to do something indefinitely until a certain condition is met, or until something else abruptly takes you out of the loop	```do { study = 'y'; readbooks = 'y'; TakeTest(pass); } while (pass == 'N')```	```Do While (pass = "N") study = "y" readbooks = "y" TakeTest(pass) Loop```
switch	This is the equivalent of a case statement or select statement in other languages. Based on the value of an integer, perform a certain action or actions. NOTE: For Palm C you cannot evaluate any variables other than integer-based ones; evaluations of character strings, floating-point numbers, etc., is not valid.	```switch(channel) { case 1: watch("ABC"); break; case 2: watch("CBS"); break; case 3: watch("NBC"); break; case 4: case 5: case 6: watch("ESPN"); default: watch("TVGuide"); break; }```	```Select Case channel Case 1 watch("ABC") Case 2 watch("CBS") Case 3 watch("NBC") Case 4, 5, 6 watch("ESPN") Case Else watch("TVGuide") End Select```

Functions

You could arguably say the entire C language is nothing but functions and you'd be, essentially, correct. A function in C takes the following form:

```
outdatatype FunctionName(parmlist)
{

    // local variables you want to declare

    // actions you want to perform

    // exit here
    return(returnvalue);

}
```

Here's a filled-out example:

```
Int16 ConvertFToC(Int16 ftemp)
{
    // local variables you want to declare
    Int16 ctemp;

    // actions you want to perform
    ctemp = (ftemp - 32) * (5 / 9);

    // exit here
    return(ctemp);

}
```

To use this function, you would simply perform it as an in-line call just like you would any other C function:

```
Int16 NYCTempF = 40;
Int16 CHITempF = 25;
Int16 AUSTempF = 80;
Int16 MIATempF = 91;

Int16 NYCTempC;
Int16 CHITempC;
Int16 AUSTempC;
Int16 MIATempC;
```

14

```
// And call the functions here....
NYCTempC = ConvertFToC(NYCTempF);
CHITempC = ConvertFToC(CHITempF);
AUSTempC = ConvertFToC(AUSTempF);
MIATempC = ConvertFToC(MIATempF);
```

As in Visual Basic and other languages, functions can have more than one parameter – or it can have none, as in this example:

```
void SayName(void)
{

    FrmCustomAlert(myAlert, "Your name is", gName, "");

}
```

In the example above, "gName" is a global character string variable that is "visible" within function SayName. All this function does is to spit out a message that says "Your name is" and the value of gName. FrmCustomAlert is a very handy function you'll be using a lot; it is a part of the Palm API (application programming interface) and you'll be seeing it again soon.

The first "void" preceding the function name SayName indicates the type of value that's returned. Also, note that in the function above, there is no "return" statement. That's because with a void function, the function doesn't return anything. The word void also appears in the parameter list because the function doesn't require anything to be passed in either. Speaking in the mathematical sense of the word this isn't truly a function because it doesn't return a value. This is actually a procedure or subroutine. But for the C language, this is a function.

Consider, on the other hand, our F-to-C temperature conversion function from page 14:

```
Int16 ConvertFToC(Int16 ftemp)
{
    Int16 ctemp;

    ctemp = (ftemp - 32) * (5 / 9);

    return(ctemp);
}
```

The "Int16" preceding the name "ConvertFToC" indicates a 16-bit integer will be returned, and that a return instruction had better be typed before that last "}". This function, in fact, has one, *ctemp*.

Pointers

Pointers are arguably the trickiest part of the C language, particularly for those who have used other languages that didn't require pointers (like Visual Basic). So let me see if I can explain this intelligently, and rationalize the reason pointers exist.

A pointer, at base level, is a memory address variable, expressed in hexadecimal (or "hex"). That's really all it is. You don't use a pointer value by itself; you use a pointer variable, and such variables are signified by an asterisk preceding the name, such as:

```
Char *icecream;
Char *milkshake;
Char *cake;
```

In the vast majority of the cases for Palm programming you'll be using either a pointer to manage either (a) a character string, or (b) a pointer to a reserved, "locked" block of memory. For right now, that's all you need to know; just accept that.

In some cases you'll see Palm API functions that require a pointer variable – that is, an *address* where a certain variable or control resides. For such cases, rather than passing in a pointer variable name you'll precede the name with the "&" symbol. The "&" means "the address of", as in this example:

```
FrmGetObjectBounds(frmP, FrmGetObjectIndex(frmP, gadgetID), &bounds);
```

This rather intimidating function call says to get the rectangular bounds of a gadget (a "gadget" is a real control in the Palm world) identified by the name "gadgetID", and pass it back to the where the *memory address* where the variable bounds is. The reason this is done is that when the C function calls FrmGetObjectBounds, each of the parameters passed in can't be changed; they are all local variables when the functions starts and when the function ends they disappear. So just passing "bounds" in wouldn't work, we need to pass in the *address* of the variable bounds.

You won't ever need to know the exact, numerical hex values of any of these memory addresses; that's what the pointers do – they keep track of them for you. So just trust them.

Summary of C vs. Visual Basic Differences

For those who like summary tables, here's another one.

Feature	Palm C	Visual Basic
Basic coding	Semi-colons everywhere Braces for blocks of code	No semi-colons No braces
Assignment statements	Several varieties, =, +=, -=, *=, /=	One kind: =

Boolean expressions (for logical constructs)	Tricky: remember to use the double-equal sign, double-AND sign and double-OR sign:
	if (x == 3)
	if (a && b)
	if (z || d)
		If x = 3
		If a And b
		If z Or d

Boolean constants	Represented by true, false, or 0x1, 0x0	Represented by True, False or -1, 0
Events	Represented by a set of constants such as penDownEvent or appStopEvent not tied to any control	Represented by a set of subroutines tied directly to specific controls such as cmdOK_Click and chkPass_Change

3. About The Palm API

Like any other situation where you're programming for a special device, Palm has its own set of special functions and data structures. To keep the scope of this book manageable, I'm not going to talk about each and every one of them, just the ones you will most likely be using. But first, a word about Palm's memory management scheme.

Palm's Wacky Memory Management Scheme

All right, maybe I'm being a bit hard on the Palm folks. After all, their original devices had very little memory – certainly not enough for the sort of sophisticated applications folks run today – and they had to figure out a way to ensure that everything stayed in its place, that the memory stayed well-behaved.

The best analogy I can come up with for this is a maid rearranging your living room when you're out for the day (or night) at work. You know how you are – you have the TV near the fireplace, the lamp near the wall and the easy chair in the middle of the room on the rug. You go away and eight hours later, the TV is next to the window, the lamp is in the middle of the room, and the chair is closer to the door. Ridiculous? Disconcerting? You bet. But Palm has to do the equivalent with its memory management routines – done under the covers – or it all falls apart.

Trust me: keep an open mind and just accept it.

Essentially, what Palm does is, when it needs a block of storage – for a character string, a number, a Boolean value – is to get it as what's called a **handle**. A handle is, at base level, just another pointer of sorts. It has a hex value similar to a pointer, but the hex value is like an ID number, and the handle itself is a specific number of consecutive bytes in memory.

I think a good analogy for this is Palm handles are like a box full of numbered vise grips. Imagine that you have this desk where you leave your student ID or driver's license in exchange for one of these vise grips. The attendant gives you a vise with a number on it – some arbitrary number – you don't care what it is, because it's not a serial number. It's just an ID number.

You take this vise and use it to pick up – I don't know – wooden planks. You'll have to open the vise wider to pick up more wooden planks, naturally. (Also, for this illustration, assume you can't pick up the wooden planks with your bare hands, either. No cheating.)

Each of those wooden planks represents a block of memory bytes. More memory is needed for storing more data items – integers, floating-point numbers, bitmaps, etc. But you have to prevent someone else from grabbing that wooden plank – someone walking by with … another vise, perhaps! Otherwise what you wind up with is a situation where two people are fighting over one wooden plank – with dueling vise grips – not a good thing.

To claim the wooden planks, you have to lock your vise. So you lock your vise – you lock your block of memory – and no other process can use it or the wooden planks you hold in your hot little hands. No one else can use it, that is, until you eventually unlock it.

The point of this convoluted illustration is this: lots of Palm processes involve handles that are associated with reserved chunks of memory ("chunks" is actually the technical term in the Palm world). When you create a memory handle, you either specify how much memory you want for a specific purpose, or you give the handle to a Palm API function for memory management and it handles the handle (sorry). For many processes you will lock the handle in order to prevent the value from changing while other things are happening, and when you do, a function will give you the hex location for that handle, represented as a C pointer (you will especially see this when you start messing around with text fields; it will take more than a few days for it to sink in if you're of average braininess). For most procedures, after you're done, you'll have to clean up by unlocking the handles and/or freeing the pointers (basically throwing them back into the bit bucket for reuse).

If you're accustomed to taking memory management for granted as you do in languages like Visual Basic, this will take quite some time to get accustomed to. But it will come to you, I promise.

Math Problems? MathLib

If all this news doesn't have your head swimming a bit, consider this: Palm has lousy floating-point support. It's so bad that you actually have to use a public-domain package called **MathLib** to work with the numbers. MathLib has all the functions you'd expect in a well-defined programming language –

trigonometric functions, logarithmic and exponential functions, roots and powers, and so on. We'll be talking more about using MathLib in Chapter 15.

Most-Used Palm API Functions

Palm API (application programming interface) functions are C functions that were originally written by the folks at PalmSource – the now-defunct development arm of Palm Corporation – to provide conveniences for those of us wanting to write Palm programs so we don't have to bonk our heads against the wall writing everything under the sun.

The following sections summarize the functions by category. For right now, don't worry about memorizing everything here. I'm not even going to give you the arguments for each function. Like learning a new language, I just want to get you accustomed to what you'll be seeing through exposure. Or, like one of my former colleagues would say, you're going to be "mentally hanging things on hooks." For my VB friends, I also mention what I would consider the closest equivalent instruction or operation.

The naming convention for Palm API functions is like this: the first two or three characters refer to the family of function – whether it applies to memory management, database management, input-output to the form, or a floating-point math function. After that, the rest of the name is, I hope, descriptive enough to tell you what you need to do. It is, often, a verb followed by a noun – for example, "Draw Form", "Open Database", "Go to Form". And so on.

Please, please, please read over **all** these functions – I don't get real specific and you will see many of them later. Develop what I call a "nodding familiarity" with them. I will not be covering absolutely all of these functions in the rest of the book; just the ones you'll likely use the most. If you see a function that I haven't covered to your satisfaction by the time you've finished this book, please look it up in Palm's extensive Help documentation (which I discuss in Chapter 17).

Form Functions

Form functions all pertain to the form, the thing on which all the controls are placed. These are the ones you'll see and use the most.

FrmCustomAlert

What It Does: Puts up a message box. You supply one, two or three arguments and it's displayed.

Closest VB Equivalent Function: MsgBog

When You'll Use It: Heavily during debugging; also for displaying messages during your Palm program.

FrmGetActiveForm

What It Does: Determines which form is active – in VB terms which form has the "focus".

Closest VB Equivalent Function: Not applicable. In VB you just refer to a control on a form without having to get the focus first.

When You'll Use It: When you need to refer to a control on a form – such as getting the value of a text field.

FrmGetObjectPtr

What It Does: Remember what I was saying about pointers in C? Here's a function that returns one as a value. This looks at a control on a form that you specify and returns a C pointer to it, a hex memory location.

Closest VB Equivalent Function: Not applicable. In VB you just refer to a control on a form by its name.

When You'll Use It: When reading a value from or setting a value to a control, usually in a text field.

FrmGetObjectIndex

What It Does: Gives the sequential number of a control on a form. Each control on a Palm form is numbered starting with 0, and going up by 1 for each additional control. This function is almost always used in conjunction with

FrmGetObjectPtr because FrmGetObjectPtr needs you to specify which numbered control you're wanting to access. Strange but true.

FrmDrawForm

What It Does: Repaints/refreshes/redraws the current form.

Closest VB Equivalent Function: Refresh.

When You'll Use It: After you have changed an object on a form, you have to have Palm repaint the whole form. It doesn't just update by itself. In VB, usually this isn't necessary.

FrmInitForm

What It Does: Loads a form into memory. Does not display it, though. Use FrmDrawForm for that.

Closest VB Equivalent Function: Load function.

When You'll Use It: When you need to bring a new form into memory.

FrmGotoForm

What It Does: Sends you to another form to display.

Closest VB Equivalent Function: Using Hide on your current form and Show on the next loaded form.

When You'll Use It: When you need to go to the next form you want.

String Functions

String functions are for manipulating character strings. Palm, however, doesn't want you to use the standard C functions like strcpy or strcompare. For some mysterious reason they want you to use their own bi-capitalized versions, so pay careful attention to the spelling differences – you'll be doing a lot of bi-capitalization of the same function names.

StrCopy

What It Does: Copies the value of one string to another.

Closest VB Equivalent Function: Any string assignment statement. (e.g. Password = "squiggle")

When You'll Use It: When you normally use an assignment statement, stop yourself and use this.

StrCat

What It Does: Attaches a second string to the "back" (or right side) of a first string.

Closest VB Equivalent Function: Any string concatentation operation, but only going from left to right. (e.g. FullName = FullName & FirstName then another statement FullName = FullName & LastName is the best approximation).

When You'll Use It: When you want to build a string.

StrCompare

What It Does: Compares one string to another and tells you which is larger or if they're equal.

Closest VB Equivalent Function: Any string comparison function (e.g. If YourGrade > MyGrade, If YourGrade < MyGrade, If YourGrade = MyGrade).

When You'll Use It: When you need to compare two strings to cause some other operation to happen (calling another function, displaying another form, etc.). The thing to get used to is that the function can return one of three values – positive 1 if the first value is greater, negative 1 if the second value is greater, and 0 if both values are identical. Most of the time you'll probably use this to see if one string is equal to another.

24

StrLen

What It Does: Tells you the length of a character string.

Closest VB Equivalent Function: Len( ) function or the Length property.

When You'll Use It: When you want to determine how long a string is.

StrATol

What It Does: Changes a string into an integer (NOTE: You cannot use this to convert into a decimal!)

Closest VB Equivalent Function: CInt( ) or Val( ) but only with an integer argument.

When You'll Use It: When you want to change a string into a numeric value. You'll do this if, for example, you have an entry field on your form where your user will enter a number as text, and to do something mathematical with it, you'll have to change it into a number first.

StrIToA

What It Does: Changes an integer into a string (opposite of StrATol).

Closest VB Equivalent Function: CStr( ) function or ToString method.

When You'll Use It: When you want to change an integer value into a string value. You'll likely use this if you need to save a number into a Palm database.

Field Functions

Field functions are for working with Palm text entry fields. If you're coming from a Windows programming language background this will seem as exotic as peacock farming but keep an open mind.

FldGetTextHandle

What It Does: Based on the pointer to the field you supply, return a memory handle (remember the locking vise?).

Closest VB Equivalent Function: There is none.

When You'll Use It: When you need to read the value of a text field control, this is one of the functions you'll use. It will likely not be the only one, though.

FldSetTextHandle

What It Does: Based on the pointer to the field you supply, set a field's value to a string pointed to by a pointer (did you follow that?).

Closest VB Equivalent Function: None.

When You'll Use It: When you want to set the value of a field, maybe to a default value, you'll use this.

FldDrawField

What It Does: Repaints the text field control. This is similar to FrmDrawForm, but for a single text field. Remember that when you change the value of a text field, you're changing it behind the scenes. You turn on the change when you give an explicit instruction to Palm to redraw the field. **This is very important, or when you run your Palm program, you'll see weird and strange behavior.**

Closest VB Equivalent Function: Refresh or Repaint methods for any control.

When You'll Use It: To update the contents of a text field.

FldGetTextPtr

What It Does: Based on the pointer to the field you supply, return another pointer to the contents of the text field. You may only use this on non-editable fields, though. This is basically the same thing as FldGetTextHandle, but you only use this for fields that the user cannot change. **Important: Use this**

function followed immediately by FldDrawField or the change won't show properly.

Closest VB Equivalent Function: The Text property of any field control.

When You'll Use It: When you need to get the value of a text field control.

FldSetTextPtr

What It Does: Based on the pointer to the field you supply, set the text field to the value of a character string pointed to by another pointer. You may only use this on non-editable fields, though. This is basically the same thing as FldSetTextHandle, but you only use this for fields that the user cannot change.

Closest VB Equivalent Function: The Text property of any field control.

When You'll Use It: When you need to set the value of a text field control. Remember, this can only be used for fields **not** marked "Editable".

FldRecalculateField

What It Does: This one's weird – this actually turns on word wrap for multi-line fields.

Closest VB Equivalent Function: None.

When You'll Use It: When you define a multi-line field as having word wrap, you can't do that at design time. You activate word wrap with this function.

Database/Data Manager Functions

Database functions are for manipulating Palm databases which, to a large extent, really are more like flat files than databases. I guess the reason Palm calls databases what they are is that most of the time, they hold data. But you could approximate the same thing with an ASCII file in Windows Notepad.

DmNewRecord

What It Does: Creates a new record – literally a spaceholder of a certain length of bytes – to a Palm database.

Closest VB Equivalent Function: Open *FileSpec* For Output As #1: Print #1, *RecordStructure*

When You'll Use It: When you're adding a new record to a database.

DmWrite

What It Does: Writes a record to the database – this is actually an I/O function.

Closest VB Equivalent Function: Open *FileSpec* For Output As #1: Print #1, *RecordStructure*

When You'll Use It: When you've put a bunch of values in a record structure and you're ready to write it to a database.

DmReleaseRecord

What It Does: Releases a record. When you create a new record or access an existing record it locks it. This function lets you release it.

Closest VB Equivalent Function: None.

When You'll Use It: When you're through with a particular record.

DmGetRecord

What It Does: Moves the contents of a database record to a memory handle so you can access each field.

Closest VB Equivalent Function: None.

When You'll Use It: When you want a particular record number, use this. Be sure to use with DmReleaseRecord.

DmQueryRecord

What It Does: Similar to DmGetRecord, except this one doesn't lock the record. So you don't have to use DmReleaseRecord with it. It's like the difference between Read-Write access and Read-Only access.

Closest VB Equivalent Function: Open *FileSpec* For Input As #1: Input #1, var1, var2, var3, etc.

When You'll Use It: When you just want to read a database record, not change it.

DmOpenDatabaseByTypeCreator

What It Does: Lets you open a database using your four-character creator ID. I'll say more about creator ID's in the section "Starting A New Project" on page 38.

Closest VB Equivalent Function: Open *FileSpec* For *AccessType* As #1

When You'll Use It: When you're ready to access a particular Palm database.

DmCreateDatabase

What It Does: Creates a new, never-before-used, database on your Palm device, dynamically.

Closest VB Equivalent Function: Open *FileSpec* For Output As #1: Print #1: Close #1 (when you close).

When You'll Use It: When your Palm application expects to find a database and can't find it, then you call this function to create it.

DmGetDatabase

What It Does: Grabs hold of a Palm database. The difference: This function grabs by serial number.

Closest VB Equivalent Function: None.

When You'll Use It: About the only time I think you'd use this is when you need to change an attribute flag on a database – things like "hidden", "copy protect", etc. More on this later, too.

DmDatabaseInfo

What It Does: Lets you read database attributes.

Closest VB Equivalent Function: None.

When You'll Use It: When you want to check a database's attributes – "hidden", "copy protect", etc.

DmSetDatabaseInfo

What It Does: Lets you change database attributes.

Closest VB Equivalent Function: None.

When You'll Use It: When you want to change a database's attributes.

DmNumRecords

What It Does: Tells you how many records are in your database (surprise, surprise).

Closest VB Equivalent Function: For an ASCII file in VB, there is no equivalent.

When You'll Use It: When you need to know how many records are in a database.

DmGetResource

What It Does: This is not a database function. This grabs what Palm calls a resource – any control, any predefined string, etc. – and returns the hex location as a pointer.

Closest VB Equivalent Function: None – VB already knows where everything is. Palm makes you point it out.

When You'll Use It: When you need to access and interact with a control, gadget, predefined string, bitmap, etc.

DmReleaseResource

What It Does: The opposite of DmGetResource – you're turning loose a locked resource.

Closest VB Equivalent Function: None.

When You'll Use It: After you're through with a resource.

DmCloseDatabase

What It Does: Closes a Palm database.

Closest VB Equivalent Function: Close #1

When You'll Use It: When you're through with a database. You must close all open databases before your Palm application shuts down or Palm gets grumpy and throws an exception that resets the device.

Memory Manager Functions

Memory manager functions are like the maid I was telling you about, the one who rearranges your living room while you're out. You call these functions and memory optimization is handled under the covers.

MemHandleNew

What It Does: Creates a new handle of a specific size (number of bytes).

Closest VB Equivalent Function: Dim (e.g., Dim n as Integer)

When You'll Use It: When you need to create a new handle, particularly when you need one for a record or a table.

MemHandleLock

What It Does: Locks a memory handle, ensuring the memory grabbed by the handle can't be changed by anyone or anything else. Returns a locked *pointer* (*not* a handle) meaning you can set the value to a character string.

Closest VB Equivalent Function: None.

When You'll Use It: Usually when you're changing the value of a text field after which point you'll use MemHandleUnlock (see below).

MemHandleUnlock

What It Does: Unlocks a memory handle.

Closest VB Equivalent Function: None.

When You'll Use It: When you're through messing around with a text field. But then you'll also need MemHandleFree (see below).

MemHandleFree

What It Does: Discards a memory handle you created; deletes a memory handle; the opposite of MemHandleNew.

Closest VB Equivalent Function: None.

When You'll Use It: After working with a text field. If you don't free memory handles when you're through with them, when your application shuts down, you get a nasty error message.

MemPtrUnlock

What It Does: Unlocks a pointer. Some pointers are locked, some aren't. Go figure.

Closest VB Equivalent Function: None.

When You'll Use It: When you've created a new record in your database and written it, this is what you'll call to release the link to the pointer variable to a C record structure. Typically used after **DmWrite** (see above).

Things You Took For Granted That You'll Need to Do Explicitly

With a Palm application you'll find yourself doing certain things more than once. Like...

Bitmap Families

When you create a bitmap, as for a game, you may not create it once. You may also have to create a "low-res" version in just two colors – black and white. You may want to create other versions in multiple shades of gray. Whatever the case, you're likely to spend a little more time creating multiple versions of a graphic image, so get used to that. Different Palm devices display graphics differently.

Event Routines

With Microsoft languages like Visual Basic, you place event code by simply double-clicking on a control. Their development environment creates the routine automatically, for you. Not so with Palm. In an event handling routine, you'll have to add new branches to a C **switch** statement. If you want a special routine to fire, you'll have to write it yourself. And when you create a new form, you'll actually have to create its own event handling routine – so you'll actually be defining a new form in two places, the controls and the event handler.

Painting and Repainting Forms

This is especially true when you're writing a Palm game but it applies to other types of applications as well. When you move a value to a text box, it won't display right away – you'll have to call **FldDrawField** to update it on screen. If you have a bitmap displayed, and go to a dialog form with the tap of a button, when you come back you'll have to redraw that bitmap. One thing that you'll want to put in the back of your mind – check the **DrawBehind** box.

4. Getting Started

The table has been set. It's time to get down to business. This chapter will show you how to download and install the Garnet OS Development Suite, give you a quick walk-through so you know your surroundings, and even – I promise – show you how to write your first Palm program!

Downloading The Garnet System

To begin, get on the World Wide Web and point your browser to:

`http://www.accessdevnet.com`

The first thing you'll have to do before downloading GDS is to join the ACCESS Developer Network program. It's free. Click on the link to register and choose a password.

Then click on the following sequence of links: **Downloads, Garnet OS Development Tools, ACCESS Tools, Garnet OS Development Suite, Full Version (178 MB)**. (If you don't have broadband or high-speed Internet service this could take quite a while, so you might consider performing the download overnight while you sleep in such a case.)

Once you've downloaded and unzipped all the files, check them with a virus scanner (always a smart thing to do!).

Cygwin – The Unix Pretender

One word about Cygwin – you may see a warning message (as a Windows dialog box) pop up, talking about using Cygwin on your system. What is Cygwin? Cygwin simulates a Unix environment and is the C compiler on which the Garnet OS Development system is based. That is all you need to know. You won't likely ever use Cygwin for anything else besides Palm development, so just know it's there and forget it.

A Tour Of The Garnet Development Suite (GDS)

When you start the Garnet Development Suite – abbreviated hereafter as *GDS* for simplicity, you'll see ACCESS' lovely splash screen shown in Figure 1.

After a few moments, you'll be presented with the main workspace screen. This is shown in Figure 2 (opposite page). At the top of the screen is the menu bar with sub-menus for **File, Edit, Navigate, Search, Project, Run, Window,** and **Help**.

Underneath the menu bar is the toolbar – a series of buttons that provide short cuts for tasks you may perform often, such as saving your project and source files, printing, and searching for text strings in your code.

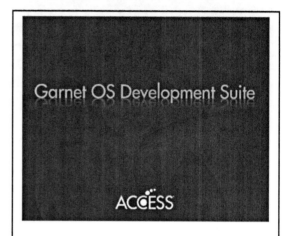

Figure 1. Garnet Development System Splash.

Notice that the workspace is divided into four windows. The white box at left is the **C/C++ Projects** window. Here, you'll see the hierarchical structure of your Palm project – files, functions, and even symbolic declarations.

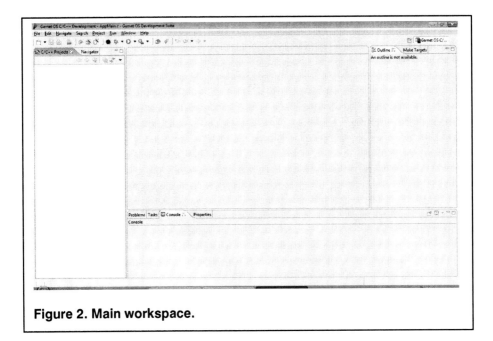

Figure 2. Main workspace.

Next to the **Projects** window, on top, is the main coding area. This is where you'll type the C instructions for your Palm project.

To the right of the main coding area is the **Outline** window. The Outline window is similar to the Project window, but presents a list of all the functions defined to your project.

Finally, underneath both those two windows is the **Console** window. This is a status area that shows what's happening when you compile your C project. You'll need to pay close attention to what's going on in this window, because if your project fails to compile, this window will offer clues as to why.

Don't worry about anything else I haven't mentioned so far. My goal is to get you coding as soon as possible, not to make you an overnight expert.

Installing Garnet Development Suite

The Garnet Development Suite can be installed on Windows computers only. There is no suite available for the Mac platform (take that, Apple).

After downloading the GDS from the ACCESS web site, you should unzip the file into a folder on your hard drive. There will only be one file, with the name:

```
Garnet OS Development Suite
Installer.exe
```

This file is approximately 184KB in size. Double-click on this file to begin the installation process, which should take about 5 minutes.

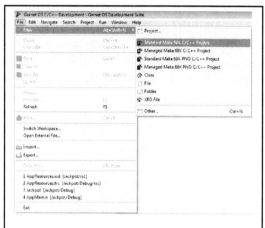

Figure 3. Creating A New Palm Project.

Starting A New Project

To write a Palm program, the first thing you need to do is to define a new project.

Step 1. Start the Garnet Development Suite by clicking on your Windows **Start** button.

Step 2. On the menu bar, choose **File → New → Standard Make 68K C/C++ Project** as shown in Figure 3. Do not concern yourself with any of the other choices.

Step 3. The **New Project** window appears, shown in Figure 4. Pick a name for your new Palm

Figure 4. New Project Window #1.

project. For your first project, type **Scorer**. Note that as you type the project name, the Project Contents' **Directory** box (grayed out but still active) underneath it is updated with the name of a new folder. After typing the project name, click the **Next** button.

Step 4. A second **New Project** window appears but with additional options.

For **Project Output**, leave **Application (prc)** as the selection; all Palm applications will have this file type. You also do not need to change the values for the entry fields Output Name without extension, Database Type, Database Name, or Database Version.

For **Creator ID**, enter a four-character code, such as "ABCD". Creator ID's uniquely identify Palm programs within your Palm device. This prevents operations from stepping all over each other. In the larger Palm universe, this also marks programs from different manufacturers. Two programs cannot share the same

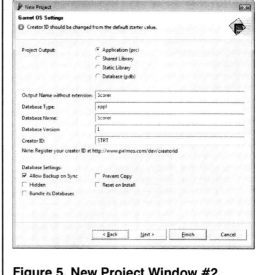

Figure 5. New Project Window #2.

Figure 6. New Project Window #3.

Creator ID. For this sample project, type **SCOR** (after which point you'll see the caution message at the top of the box disappear). Then click the **Next** button.

Step 5. The last step in this multi-part process is to choose a starter application, or an application structure. Click on **Simple Application** to select it (Figure 6). The Simple Application is a bare-bones project that prints out nothing than the traditional first program message, "Hello, world!". If

39

you're curious, later, you can define another project and choose *Sample Application*; this creates a sliding tile puzzle. But for our purposes right now, click on **Simple Application**, and then click the **Finish** button. GDS whirs and clicks, generating files, and after a few moments you'll be presented with the workspace again, but this time, with the name of the project in the C/C++

Projects window (Figure 7).

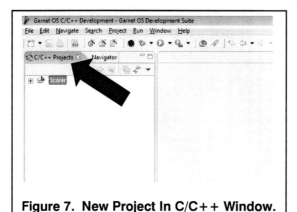

Figure 7. New Project In C/C++ Window.

Overview Of A Palm C Project

Click the [+] button next to the name of our project, Scorer. As in Windows' File Explorer, this opens up the next levels of the "tree" (shown in Figure 8).

You'll notice there are two parent nodes in this tree, **rsc** and **src**. The node "rsc" stands for **resources**, while "src" stands for **source code**.

Figure 8. Project Hierarchy.

Resources are all the controls, objects and graphics that are used to make a Palm program run. Resources include buttons, sliders, tabs, text fields, labels and bitmaps. **Source code** is all the C instructions that use and manipulate the resources to make a Palm program operate. It includes sets of instructions to start the program, display a form, check for input from the Graffiti pad or buttons, detect a clock tick, or stop the program.

Do not concern yourself with the **Sections.def**, **makefile**, or **makefile-engine.mk** nodes shown. These files are critical to the operation of a Palm project, but for the level of simplicity I'm trying to convey, I'm not going to explain them. Leave them alone.

Let's expand both of the **rsc** and **src** levels. Click the [+] button next to each, one at a time.

Underneath rsc, you can now see a node called **bitmaps**, with a single node called **AppResources.xrd** underneath it. The bitmaps node is a folder containing, as you can imagine, bitmaps. This includes icons for the Palm program.

Figure 9. RSC and SRC Nodes.

AppResources.xrd is a file pointing to all the resources including the bitmaps. When you double-click on this node, it'll open up a special editor for the Palm controls (buttons, bitmaps, text fields, etc.). More on that later in this book.

Underneath src, there are three nodes with their own tree structures underneath them. They are **AppResources.h**, **Sections.h**, and **AppMain.c**.

41

The only file we'll be changing is **AppMain.c**. The other two nodes, as is known by any experienced C programmer, are C **header files** – or predefined instructions, constants and functions. You will not need to change the header files, ever.

Organization Of A Palm C Program

Now that you've had a quick tour of the editing environment, let's take a look at how a Palm C program is organized. Remember, this is just for you to get acquainted, not to memorize everything. As you get into the process of writing code, you'll start to recognize the pattern of the code.

Double click on the **AppMain.c** node of the C/C++ Projects tree. This will open the main program module and the work area and Outline sections will fill in, as shown in Figure 10 below.

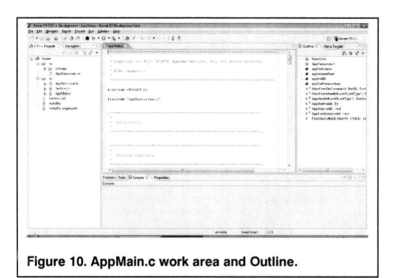

Figure 10. AppMain.c work area and Outline.

At the top of the AppMain.c code file, you'll see the following two lines after the prologue:

```
#include <PalmOS.h>
#include "AppResources.h"
```

As mentioned a couple of pages back, these two lines represent C header files. Don't ever delete these two lines or you'll be in a world of trouble; they contain important Palm routines, functions and constants.

Scroll down a little bit, and you'll see a banner header reading:

```
/**********************************************************************
 *
 *  Entry Points
 *
 **********************************************************************/
```

Don't concern yourself with this section; you won't be adding any entry points, which is well beyond the scope of this book.

Underneath that section, you'll see the **Internal Constants** section:

```
/**********************************************************************
 *
 *  Internal Constants
 *
 **********************************************************************/
#define appFileCreator          'SCOR'
#define appVersionNum           0x01
#define appPrefID               0x00
#define appPrefVersionNum       0x01
```

Internal Constants are where Palm defines some variables (effectively) that serve as constants. Elsewhere in the Palm architecture these values are used so the not-so-friendly values (0x01, 0x00) don't have to be used. At some point, you'll be defining your own constants in this manner, using the **#define** instruction.

Following the Internal Constants section, you have the **Internal Functions** section:

```
/**********************************************************************
 *
 *  Internal Functions
 *
 **********************************************************************/
```

This section has a set of predefined functions that make up a typical Palm program. It is also a section you will be expanding with your own functions.

One important thing to remember about Palm C functions: you must define the function "higher" in the code before you use it. Palm C programs are compiled in a one-pass fashion. If you reference a function name before it has been declared, the Palm compiler will shrug its shoulders and go, "What?"

Now let's look at the functions one at a time, but to do this, scroll all the way to the bottom of AppMain.c. We're going to scroll upwards, working our way *upwards* in the calling hierarchy. C programs are kind of upside down this way; we'll be looking at the very highest calling program first. In this way, the structure of the Palm program will make more sense.

PilotMain

The **PilotMain** function is always part of any Palm C program. Its main function is to ensure a Palm program starts normally, and if it does, it calls two other functions which you can see in the code:

```
AppEventLoop();
AppStop();
```

You can use the PilotMain function to stop a program if some prerequisite has not been met – e.g., too early a version of the Palm OS is running.

AppEventLoop

Scrolling upwards, you see the definition for **AppEventLoop**, which was called by PilotMain. AppEventLoop is a function that, essentially, does one thing – sits and waits for something to happen.

AppEventLoop is a loop that does five things:

- Gets the next waiting event with **EvtGetEvent**

- Checks for a system-level event with **SysHandleEvent**

- Checks for a menu-level event with **MenuHandleEvent**

- Checks for an application-level event with **AppHandleEvent**

- If none of the three events above has happened, process the current form using **FrmDispatchEvent**.

The loop continues to run continuously, infinite-loop fashion, until there's a "stop" event, shown by this Boolean condition:

```
while (event.eType != appStopEvent)
```

That is all this single function does. It's quite simple, but very important, as it is run hundreds and thousands of times a Palm application is active.

AppStop

As you can imagine, **AppStop** is called when you leave a program by tapping another button, press a key on the Palm unit, or power the unit off. It calls a single Palm API function, **FrmCloseAllForms**. Except on rare occasions, you will probably not need to change this function much.

AppStart

AppStart, naturally, is the analogue to AppStop. AppStart is called when a Palm program is starting up. As with AppStop, this one also calls a single Palm API function, **FrmGotoForm**, with a parameter MainForm. "MainForm" is a constant representing the value 1000, which serves as an identification number for the main form. Typically, the first definition of any new form, button, bitmap, control, etc., has the number 1000. This is merely a coding convention, not a requirement. You will be able to assign ID numbers in any manner you choose, even starting with the number 1 if you like, but you may find it preferable to stick to Palm's coding convention to give you some structure.

AppHandleEvent

As we continue our upward scrolling trek, we come to **AppHandleEvent**. This function was called "lower" in the code by **AppEventLoop** (see above). This function is the most complex one we've looked at yet; let's take a closer look:

```
if (pEvent->eType == frmLoadEvent) {

    // Load the form resource.
    formId = pEvent->data.frmLoad.formID;

    pForm = FrmInitForm(formId);
    FrmSetActiveForm(pForm);

    // Set the event handler for the form.  The handler of the currently
    // active form is called by FrmHandleEvent each time is receives an
    // event.
    switch (formId) {
        case MainForm:
            FrmSetEventHandler(pForm, MainFormHandleEvent);
            break;

        default:
            break;
    }
    handled = true;
}

return handled;
```

The first thing the function does is to look at a data structure called **pEvent**. pEvent, for this function, points to a variable called **eType**. pEvent is continually updated by the Palm processor; when a new event takes place – such as a tap on the Graffiti pad – event data are dumped into the pEvent data structure. (Again, don't worry about the details of this; just take for granted that this happens.)

On this line:

```
if (pEvent->eType == frmLoadEvent) {
```

AppHandleEvent is checking to see if an event to load a form (**frmLoadEvent**, a constant) has taken place. Most of the time, this will not be the case – once a form is loaded, it stays loaded until the user either goes to another form or leaves the program completely.

So if a form load event has happened, a series of special instructions is performed. First, there's:

```
// Load the form resource.
formId = pEvent->data.frmLoad.formID;
```

This instruction grabs the form ID number (in this case, 1000) and assigns it to a local variable **formId**. Next there's:

```
pForm = FrmInitForm(formId);
FrmSetActiveForm(pForm);
```

Here we call another Palm API function, **FrmInitForm**, with the value of 1000 stored in the pointer variable **formId**. (Palm could just as easily have passed the numerical value 1000, but when you begin dealing with multiple forms or controls, you'll appreciate why to use variable and constant names rather than numbers.) **FrmInitForm** initializes (or loads) a form. (In Visual Basic it could be thought of as the equivalent of the Form_Load event.) The result of this operation is sent to a pointer variable called **pForm**.

The line underneath uses the pointer variable pForm to call another Palm API function, **FrmSetActiveForm**. FrmSetActiveForm calls the focus to the main form or, in other words, activates it. It's basically the same as saying, "Okay, Palm, I want you to use *this* form now."

Underneath these two instructions you have a switch construct based on the variable **formId** which is the ID number for the main form:

46

```
// Set the event handler for the form.  The handler of the currently
// active form is called by FrmHandleEvent each time is receives an
// event.
switch (formId) {
    case MainForm:
        FrmSetEventHandler(pForm, MainFormHandleEvent);
        break;

    default:
        break;
}
```

Right now, there's not much there. Since there's only one form in this Palm project, there's just one form ID (**MainForm**, which has the value 1000) to check for. Otherwise, nothing is done (the default leg of the switch).

Note that if the MainForm is detected, there's a call to Palm API function **FrmSetEventHandler**. Every form that you define to a Palm C program must have its own dedicated event handler. This is not as complicated as it sounds, though; most of the time you'll just make a copy of an existing FrmSetEventHandler function and paste it underneath an existing one.

The function FrmSetEventHandler has two parameters. The first is the pointer to the form (the pointer variable **pForm**). The second is the name of another function, **MainFormHandleEvent**. There is nothing special about naming event handlers, but to help you keep things straight, I suggest you use Palm's convention of naming event handlers "*your-name*-HandleEvent" until you're thoroughly comfortable with the code.

Before we go looking for MainFormHandleEvent, note this last line in the function:

```
handled = true;
```

You'll see that line of code a lot, particularly in **switch** constructs throughout Palm processing. It tells Palm's event handlers, "Okay, I got it" or "This event has been processed; you don't have to wait on it anymore."

MainFormHandleEvent

We're almost near the bottom of the calling hierarchy with **MainFormHandleEvent**. This function was called by AppHandleEvent, which I discussed in the previous section. Here, once again, we have a **switch** construct, but this one is a little different:

```
switch (pEvent->eType) {
    case menuEvent:
        return MainFormDoCommand(pEvent->data.menu.itemID);

    case frmOpenEvent:
        pForm = FrmGetActiveForm();
        FrmDrawForm(pForm);
        handled = true;
        break;

    default:
        break;
}
```

This switch evaluates our event data structure, pEvent, and the variable eType rather than the formId. And as you can guess from the names on each of the **case** legs, there are two events being detected: when the menu control is tapped (**menuEvent**), and when the form is opened (**frmOpenEvent**). (Note that menuEvent and frmOpenEvent are constants defined in one of the Palm header files, the files with names ending with ".h").

The menuEvent leg calls a locally-defined function, **MainFormDoCommand**. This is not a Palm API function, but is one that is created when you define a new Palm project. It's called with our event data structure pEvent once again, but with the value **itemID**.

What does this mean? Menu options, like everything else in the Palm environment, is identified by a 4-digit integer. The first option on a drop-down menu is usually 1000; the second, 1100, and so on. When the user taps a menu, menu information is dumped to the event data structure pEvent, and in this case, that includes a **menu.itemID** number. That menu option number is sent directly to the MainFormDoCommand function (the last function which I cover in the next section) to perform whatever action is needed.

In the case a form is opened with detection of the frmOpenEvent constant, you have this first instruction:

```
pForm = FrmGetActiveForm();
```

This calls Palm API function **FrmGetActiveForm** and sends the returned pointer to the variable pForm to hold it. Next, we call a Palm API function to draw the form:

```
FrmDrawForm(pForm);
```

FrmDrawForm draws to the Palm device screen the form identified by the pointer variable you pass in. (In Visual Basic or even Java, it would be the same thing as calling a Paint event.) And finally, we have our instruction to say it's been taken care of:

```
handled = true;
```

You will define one form handler for each form you use in your Palm program.

MainFormDoCommand

Finally, as deep into the hierarchy as we get for a new Palm program, we have **MainFormDoCommand**. Again, this is not a Palm API function, but is one that is associated specifically with the main form for this application. You will be defining one of these functions for each form you design, if you add more forms to your Palm program.

Here, again, we have a pared down switch structure:

```
switch (command) {
    case MainOptionsAboutStarterApp:
        pForm = FrmInitForm(AboutForm);
        FrmDoDialog(pForm);       // Display the About Box.
        FrmDeleteForm(pForm);
        handled = true;
        break;
}
```

Recall that for MainFormDoCommand, Palm looks at the menu ID passed in. Elsewhere in the Palm code, the constant **MainOptionsAboutStarterApp** has the value 1000. When the menu option ID 1000 is passed in, three main instructions are performed.

First, a form is initialized using the Palm API function **FrmInitForm**. This time, though, it is not the MainForm constant that is passed in, but a second constant **AboutForm** that is passed instead. AboutForm has the integer value 1100. The result of this call is returned to the local pointer variable **pForm**.

Next, the Palm API function **FrmDoDialog** is called with the pointer variable pForm. FrmDoDialog displays a dialog much like a Windows program, and a Palm dialog keeps focus until it's dismissed (usually by pressing an OK button).

49

And last, once we're through displaying the form and the user has dismissed it, we get rid of it with the function **FrmDeleteForm**. This way, unused forms don't just sit in memory as orphans, taking up precious space.

As with other switch constructs you've observed, we have the **handled = true** at the end of the case leg.

So let's take a look at the whole structure, right-side-up, with the diagram in Figure 11 on the next page.

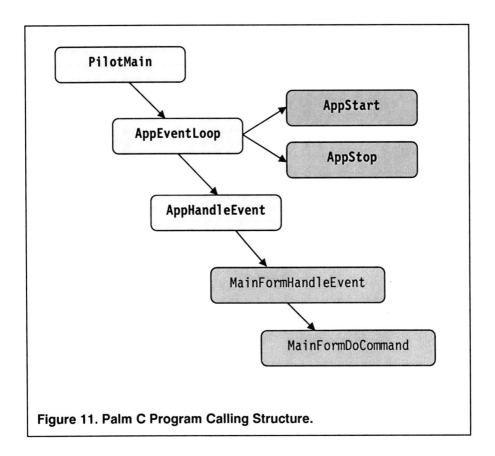

Figure 11. Palm C Program Calling Structure.

The top of the structure is standard function PilotMain, which calls standard function AppEventLoop. AppEventLoop can fire either AppStart (if a program is starting) or AppStop (if one is ending). Otherwise, it calls AppHandleEvent. AppHandleEvent, in turn, calls the functions in the blue boxes, MainFormHandle-Event, and MainFormDoCommand.

When you start writing your own Palm programs you will be defining additional "___HandleEvent" and "___DoCommand" functions yourself.

Compiling The Sample Palm Program

What? Compiling already? We haven't even written a single line of code! Not to worry – I think you'll have a better feel for the fact that this stuff actually works if you can try the sample program for yourself.

The sample program is the traditional (for students of computer science, anyway) "Hello, World" program. All it does is to display a single form with the greeting "Hello, World!" If you choose the single menu option, another form is opened that gives "About" style information. It's not sophisticated, of course, but it allows you to verify that the Palm compiler is working properly. In the following section, with this compiled sample program, I will show you how to run it in the Garnet OS Simulator.

So while the program is called "Scorer" at this point, we're going to build on it throughout the course of this book. But for now it will simply read "Hello, World!"

Step 1. On the menu bar, choose **Project**, then **Build All** (Figure 12). Then watch the Console (the window at the bottom of the screen). A window pops up called Building Workspace, and this shows the progress as the program is compiled. Compilation should take no longer than 30 seconds.

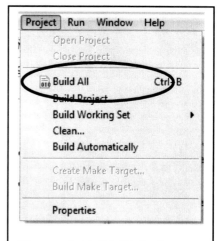

Figure 13. Build All Option.

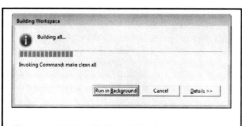

Figure 12. Building Workspace.

Step 2. Now look at the Console at the bottom of the screen in the long window. It should look like this with the **"...done..."** message at the end shown in Figure 14.

Figure 14. Console Showing Successful Compilation.

Now it's time to run this program!

Running The Sample Program

Step 1. To run the sample program which we, for the time being, have called "Scorer", return to your Windows desktop and locate the **Garnet OS Simulator** icon (or locate the option from your computer's Start menu). Start the simulator.

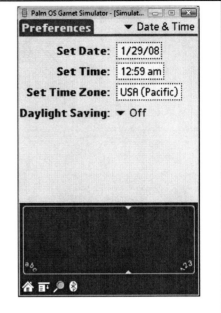

Figure 15. Garnet OS Simulator.

After a few moments the simulator will show a screen that you might see if you ever did a soft reset of your Palm device (Figure 15). The date and time are based on your computer's system clock.

Step 2. Since we can't use HotSync to send a program to this virtual device, we have to *simulate* the installation process. Right-click on the screen area and you'll see a pop-up menu with the options Reset, View, Install, etc. Select **Install** and move your mouse to the right over the selection arrow. A submenu will appear with the option **Database**. Click on the option Database and you'll see another pop-up window with the title **Install Database**.

Step 3. Locate the folder containing the Palm project you created. Remember that you defined it to a folder called **Scorer**, so look for that folder first. Once you find it, choose Debug and there will be a file with the name **Scorer.prc** (as shown in Figure 16). Click on the file name Scorer.prc and then click the **Open** button.

Step 4. Once you have selected the file, the virtual Palm device will change and you'll see the icon screen displaying the single Palm program you installed, Scorer (Figure 17). With your mouse, position the cursor over the Scorer icon (which, for the moment is a blue dot because we haven't defined an icon for it yet) and click. The Scorer application starts and (wonderfully!) you are presented with the image shown in Figure 18, a working Palm program.

You have just created your first Palm program! Congratulations!

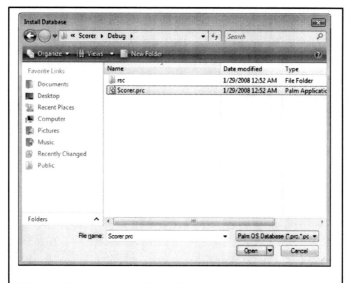

Figure 16. Locating Your Compiled Palm Program (Windows Vista).

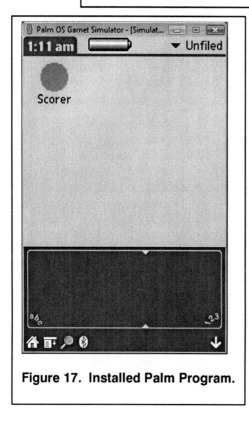

Figure 17. Installed Palm Program.

Figure 18. Running Palm Program.

To see the "About" screen for this Palm application, tap the Menu icon (near the lower left corner of the virtual Graffiti pad, next to the Home icon).

To stop the program, tap the Home icon (lower left corner).

To restart the program, simply tap the Scorer icon (blue dot) again.

A Few Words About GDS And Windows Vista

At the time this book was originally published, Windows Vista was the latest version of the Microsoft Windows operating system. Many other users were still using (actually clinging to) Windows XP.

You may observe differences in the operation of the Garnet OS Development System that are a little different under Vista, and which may require some different or additional actions in order to be able to compile your programs.

In addition, you may observe some behaviors running GDS and the Garnet OS Simulator that differ from Windows XP. When a program fails to work as you expect, you may be bewildered as to whether the problem is with Vista or with GDS which, I happen to know from experience, has a few bugs in it.

Some of the program code in this book may not be the most elegant, but was written as a workaround for irregularities that I perceived when creating and testing the projects. In some cases, a dozen lines of code may need to be written to equate with a Palm API function that you expect should work a certain way but doesn't. Your own experience, of course, may vary from mine.

Fixing The "Multiple Target Patterns" Error Message

When using GDS to create a Palm executable, you may occasionally see the following messages:

```
make clean all
Debug/rsc/AppResources.d:1: *** multiple target patterns.  Stop.
```

I have found that this is one of Vista's incompatibilities with GDS, and it pertains to one file in particular, the **make.exe** that compiles the source code. Follow the instructions below to resolve this issue.

1. Go to SourceForge's Minimalist GNU project web site at:

```
http://sourceforge.net/project/downloading.php?groupname=mingw&filename=
mingw32-make-3.80.0-3.exe&use_mirror=superb-west
```

You'll be asked to confirm you wish to download. Provided you have good anti-virus software, this shouldn't bother you.

2. Install the software, which takes a few seconds.

3. Go to your **Cygwin bin** directory, which should be **C:PalmOSCygwin/bin** and locate the **make.exe** file. Rename this file to something you'll remember (like make_original.exe).

4. Go to the folder where you installed the Minimalist GNU **make.exe** file. It will have the name **mingw32-make.exe**. Make a copy of the file and give the new file the name **make.exe**.

5. Copy the **make.exe** file into your **Cygwin/bin** directory, which should be **C:PalmOSCygwin/bin**.

6. Pull up the file manager (**Computer → Explore**) and go to the **C:PalmOSCygwin/bin** folder. Right-click on the **make.exe** file from step 5 and choose **Properties**. Click the **Compatibility** tab and choose "**XP Service Pack 2**". Click OK or Apply to save it.

7. Start the ACCESS Garnet Development Suite.

8. Create a project (**File → New → Standard Make 68K Project**, then follow the windows and screen prompts). Add the code you wish and press **Ctrl+S** to save the changes.

9. To compile, press **Ctrl+B**. This will build your project.

10. When you need to compile for the second, third, etc. time, on the **C/C++ Projects** tab (near upper left corner of screen, under the menu bar), open the **Debug** part of the "tree" so it shows everything. You'll see another tree node labeled "**rsc**" (standing for resources). **Press and hold the Ctrl key down** and **click on each of the files shown**; there will be five or six with names like **AppResources.d, AppResources.trc, AppMain.d, AppMain.o**, and so on.

11. After deleting the files, to re-compile, press **Ctrl+B** to do a clean compile. This will rebuild your project. Repeat Steps 9 and 10 as often as you need to until your Palm program is as you like.

    This is, admittedly, a bit of a hassle to make GDS play nicely with Vista. But the reality is that with Windows XP on the way out (this book was completed after Microsoft's "drop dead" date for retail sales of XP), Windows Vista will be the new standard operating system. (And, to my knowledge, there is no equivalent GDS for the Mac OS platform.) The better you learn how to run GDS under Vista, the better off you'll be.

5.   Form Design & Controls

Now that you know how something about to create a new project, compile and run it, we move on to the fun stuff – designing what's on the form itself. In this chapter I'll help you take your first steps toward placing controls in the main area of your application.

Palm Resource Editor

If you haven't already opened GDS and your Scorer project, please do so now. Since you left the Scorer project open when you exited GDS, it will automatically be there for you.

In the **C/C++ Projects** window, locate the **AppResources.xrd** node and double-click on it (Figure 19). This will start the **Palm OS Resource Editor**, shown in Figure 20. The Resource Editor is for creating and modifying all the controls in your Palm application – labels, text fields, buttons, and so on. You'll be using the Resource Editor often so we're going to get you familiar with it now.

As with the main GDS program, the Resource Editor screen is broken into several areas. The largest part of the screen, currently dark gray, is where you'll see resources appear for editing. At far right, on top, is the **Files** tree, which shows all the resources you have defined, grouped by type of resource. When you first start a

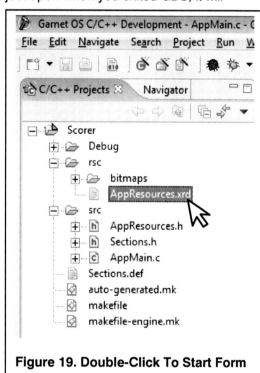

Figure 19. Double-Click To Start Form Designer.

59

new Palm program, the only resources defined are App Icon Bitmap, App Icon Name String, Form, and Menu Bar.

The **App Icon Bitmap** folder has currently defined an application icon as a blue that dot you saw in the simulator because we have not created a specific icon for it yet.

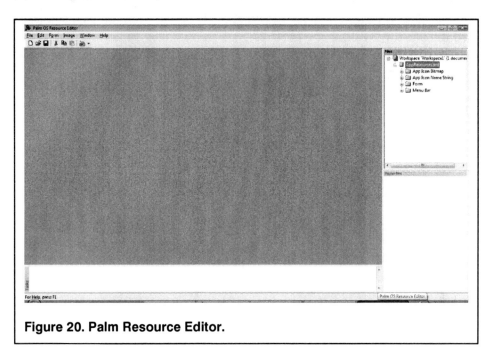

Figure 20. Palm Resource Editor.

All the **App Icon Name String** folder contains is a special string definition for the application name that appears on the Palm device menu. For this application, it simply says "Scorer". Since this is set when you create a new application, you'll typically never need to change it, so just ignore this.

The **Form** folder contains the forms a Palm application uses. Click on the [+] in front of the word "Form" and you'll see two forms already defined, numbered 1000

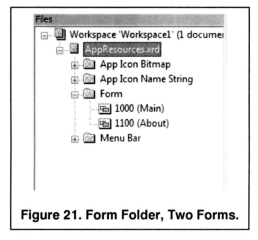

Figure 21. Form Folder, Two Forms.

and 1100. Note also that each has a description in parentheses – for 1000, it's "Main" and for 1100, it's "About". You'll want to use descriptive reminders like this when you create your own forms.

Next, we're going to open up the Main form, number 1000, and add a few controls. Double-click on the node marked **1000 (Main)**. You should see what's shown in Figure 22.

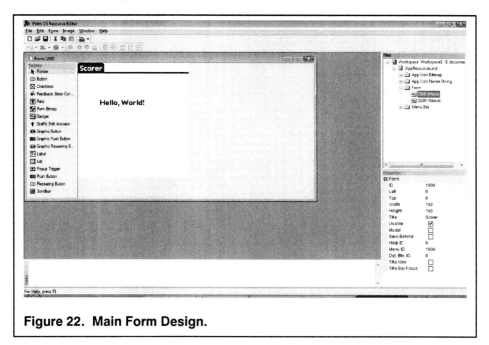

Figure 22. Main Form Design.

Palm Form Controls

In the main work area, you see a window with "Form 1000" in the title bar. Each time you open a resource definition, it opens a work window like this. Because this is a form we're editing, at left you see a column labeled "**Toolbox**" with a series of buttons underneath it ("Pointer", "Button", "Checkbox", etc.). Those are all the controls you can place on a form. Although we're going to be starting small, I'm going to give you a rundown on what each of the controls is and does, since you've probably seen them in Palm applications by this point anyway.

For the scope of this book, the controls we will be concerning ourselves with will be Button, Checkbox, Field, Form Bitmap (or just "Bitmap"), and Label. The other controls you can research yourself in other, more advanced books.

Tool Name	What It's For
Button	Basic multi-purpose control you can use for anything.
Checkbox	Just like in Windows – lets you choose which options you want.
Feedback Slider Control	Used to choose a value within a certain range.
Field	Text entry or output display.
Form Bitmap	A bitmap; any graphic element.
Gadget	A user-definable control.
Graffiti Shift Indicator	Shows whether Graffiti shift is on or not.
Graphic Button	Same as button, but with a bitmap rather than text.
Graphic Push Button	Like a Windows radio button; lets you choose one value from a set of choices. Includes graphics.
Graphic Repeating Button	Similar to Repeating Button below, but with a bitmap.
Label	Identifier for a text entry field.
List	Contains a set of values for user to select from.
Popup Trigger	Usually used with List for displaying a list.
Push Button	Like a Windows radio button; lets you choose one value from a set of choices. Text only.
Repeating Button	Button that you can tap and hold down.
Scrollbar	Control for letting you scroll up and down a field or other control.

Table 1. Palm Form Controls.

Deleting A Control

For our Scorer project, we won't be needing that "Hello, World!" string on the form. So we need to delete it. The way to delete a control on a Palm form is:

Step 1. Position your cursor over the control and click on it to select it.

Step 2. Press the **Delete** key on your keyboard.

Let's do this now. Move your cursor over the label "Hello, World!" on the form and click it. The blue dots around the border indicate that this control has been selected (shown in Figure 23).

Now press the **Delete** key on your keyboard. The label disappears. You now have a completely clear form with just the title bar that reads the name of the program, "Scorer".

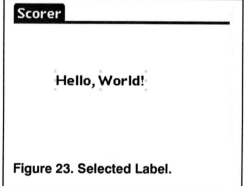

Figure 23. Selected Label.

Adding A Control

Adding a control to a Palm form is also simple:

Step 1. In the Toolbox, click the button for the type of control you wish to add.

Step 2. Position your cursor somewhere on the form, then click and drag to create the control at the size you want. (This is similar to Visual Studio programming languages.)

We are going to add two text fields and two buttons to the form.

Exercise A

Step 1. In the **Toolbox**, click on the **Field** button.

Step 2. Position your cursor about halfway down the screen, and click and drag to create a field (Figure 24).

Step 3. Repeat Step 2, but to the right of the field you created before.

Step 4. Back in the **Toolbox**, click on the **Button** button.

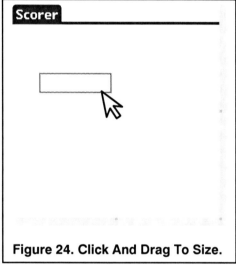

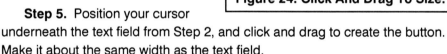

Figure 24. Click And Drag To Size.

Step 5. Position your cursor underneath the text field from Step 2, and click and drag to create the button. Make it about the same width as the text field.

Step 6. Repeat Step 5, but to the right of the button you created before.

If you've done these steps correctly, your form should like the one in Figure 25.

Now, click on each of the controls you placed and watch the **Properties** window in the lower right portion of the screen. You'll see the ID number change from 1000, to 1001, to 1002, to 1003, depending on which of the controls you've selected. You will also observe that the properties displayed will differ depending on the type of control you have selected. The text field controls have more properties than the button controls.

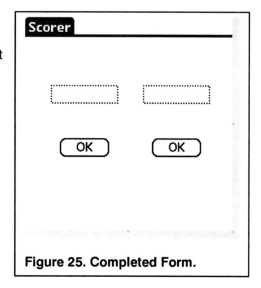

Figure 25. Completed Form.

Changing A Control's Properties

The Properties area is not just for displaying the properties of the controls; you can also change properties, too. Properties comprise all the appearance attributes, dimensions and behaviors associated with a particular control.

For example, note that both of the buttons you defined say "OK", the default. We are going to change them to say "Add L" and "Add R" in the next exercise.

Exercise B

Step 1. Click on the left side button you created in Exercise A.

Step 2. Go to the Properties window and locate the property called "Text". It's near the bottom of the list and currently has a value of "OK".

Step 3. Double-click on the right column where "OK" is shown, then back-space and type "**Add L**" instead. Press **Enter** when you're done.

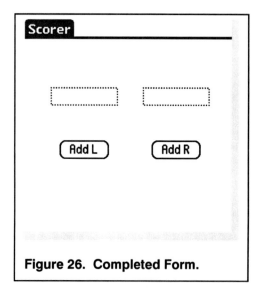

Figure 26. Completed Form.

Step 4. Repeat Steps 1 through 3, but for the button on the right. This time, type "Add R" for that button's text.

If you've performed the steps correctly, your form should appear as the one shown in Figure 26.

Now would be a good time to save your project, compile it, and try running it using the Garnet Simulator to check your progress.

Assigning Actions To Buttons

Now that we have a basic design for this application, we need to make those buttons do something. That is the purpose of this section. When it's over, you will know something about adding code to a button control. Take your time in this section, and don't skip any steps, no matter how eager you are. The Garnet OS Simulator and your Palm device won't "care" if you're anxious to rush your progress; the programs simply won't work if you're not careful.

To summarize the basic steps for adding actions to a button:

- **Decide what actions you want the button to perform.**

- **Determine what C statements are needed for those actions.**

- **Modify the event handler routine to allow the form to detect that a control has been tapped as well as to indicate which control.**

- **Define a new C function to handle the actions, containing the statements you determined are necessary.**

- **Add a function call to the event handler code with the name of your new C function.**

That, essentially, is what you do. In the next exercise we're going to add code to allow us to test that the buttons work.

Exercise C

Start your GDS if you haven't already. It will open to the Scorer project we've been working on.

Step 1. Double-click on the **AppResources.xrd** node in the C/C++ Projects window. This will open the Palm OS Resource Editor.

Step 2. Under **Files** (right half of the screen), click on the [+] button in front of the word Form in the file tree.

Step 3. Double-click on **1000 (Main)** to open the main form. The form with the two text fields and two buttons will appear.

Step 4. Click on the button you labeled "Add L". Under **Properties**, look at the value in the Control field; it should be **1002**.

Step 5. Click on the button you labeled "Add R". Under **Properties**, look at the value in the Control field; it should be **1003**.

The values 1002 and 1003 are the ID numbers associated with the controls, but we're going to create constants that will be easier to remember.

Step 6. In Windows, tab back until you're back at the GDS window. Leave the Palm OS Resource Editor open. Scroll all the way to the top of the **AppMain.c** file then look for the section labeled **"Internal Constants"**. There, you'll see four constants Palm has already defined for this program. We are going to define two more, and a couple more later.

Step 7. After the fourth **#define** statement, type the following new lines:

```
#define txtScoreL 1000        // Left Score
#define txtScoreR 1001        // Right Score
#define btnAddL 1002          // Left Add Button
#define btnAddR 1003          // Right Add Button
```

The top line says to assign the value 1000 to the constant **txtScoreL**, the second one under that says to assign the value 1001 to the constant **txtScoreR**, and so on. Now, elsewhere in the code, rather than typing 1000 or 1003 to mean the left score or the right button, you can use the more intelligent names you see here. Note that reminder comments follow the "//" marks at the end of the line, a good practice.

A word about the naming convention you'll see in this book: you will notice that the start of each control name that we use (as opposed to the ones Palm uses) begin with a lower-case abbreviation indicating what kind of data object we're using, followed by a sufficiently descriptive name. Buttons' names will begin with "btn"; forms' names will begin with "frm", text fields' names will begin with "txt", and so on. This is a common practice in programming that helps the programmer remember what data type is associated with a particular control. It is not necessary to add a prefix to variables used within a function – such as for looping with names like n, j, or k.

You are not obligated to use this naming convention; the Palm compiler doesn't care. But you may find adapting a consistent naming convention will be helpful once you have completed work on a program, put it down for a while, and pick it back up again later. You will not remember what goes on in your programs forever!

Your Internal Constants section should look like this:

```
/**********************************************************************
 *
 *   Internal Constants
 *
 **********************************************************************/
#define appFileCreator              'SCOR'
#define appVersionNum               0x01
#define appPrefID                   0x00
#define appPrefVersionNum           0x01

#define btnAddL 1002                // Left Add Button
#define btnAddR 1003                // Right Add Button
```

To test the buttons, we're going to use an alert. An **alert** is the same as a Message Box in Windows, and has the same name in JavaScript. In Palm, though, an alert must be defined as a resource – as a control to be called with a C instruction.

Step 8. In Windows, tab back to the **Palm OS Resource Editor**. Under Files, click on the **AppResources.xrd** node so it's highlighted.

Step 9. Right-click on the **AppResources.xrd** node (Figure 27)

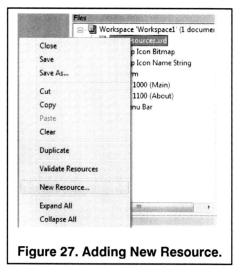

Figure 27. Adding New Resource.

and a pop-up menu appears. Choose **New Resource…** which is near the bottom of the list of options. This will open a window titled **New Resource**. Note all the different kinds of things you can define. Fortunately for us, an **Alert** is at the top of the list. Do not change either of the checkboxes at the bottom of the window; just click on **New**.

Step 10. Note that the Palm OS Resource Editor opens a new window for the alert we're going to create. And in the Files tree off to the right, at the top, there is now an "Alert" node in the tree, along with the number 1000 – this is the alert resource we just created. All of this is shown in Figure 28 below.

We are going to change the title and text of this alert.

Step 11. Under the Properties section, go to the line marked "Title" and double-click in the box, then select all the text, and then type "*Scorer Message*". Then press the **Enter** key.

Step 12. Next, go to the line marked "Message" and double-click in the box, then select all the text, and

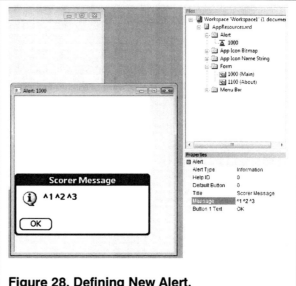

Figure 28. Defining New Alert.

then type the characters "^1 ^2 ^3". Then press the **Enter** key.

If you've done the steps correctly, your alert should like the one in Figure 28, with a single space between "^1" and "^2", and between "^2" and "^3".

What are these funny code sequences? Each of them are placeholders. What you've actually defined is called a **Custom Alert**. Rather than having a fixed message, with this style of alert, we can change the message dynamically, and there are three spaces we can fill.

It has long been my practice to use custom alerts in my Palm software development. You can use them to display intermediate status messages as well as messages to the user of your program. In addition, when you are trying to debug a program on an actual Palm device (such as a Palm T|X) you won't have a Garnet OS Simulator running – it will be the real thing! The use of custom alerts can help you detect problems on an actual device or even flag unexpected errors. I highly recommend the use of custom alerts.

Step 13. Now that we've created a new resource, let's go back and create a constant for it. Recall that this new alert was assigned the value 1000 by Palm (Palm assigns numbers sequentially by increments of 100). Go back to the GDS window, the code section, locate the "Internal Constants" section, and add this line after the other two #define lines you typed before:

```
#define myAlert 1000                    // My Alert
```

One thing to remind you about – Palm C is **case-sensitive**. You can type "MyAlert" or "MYALERT" if you prefer, but be sure that's how you type it throughout your program, for every single instance of the name.

Step 14. Press **Ctrl+S** to save your changes and close the Palm OS Resource Editor. Then return to the GDS window.

Step 15. Scroll down in the code to the **MainFormHandleEvent** function. Note that there are two case legs. We are going to add a third. After the case **frmOpenEvent** leg, type the following:

```
case ctlSelectEvent:
    switch (pEvent->data.ctlSelect.controlID) {
        case btnAddL:
            FrmCustomAlert(myAlert, "Left", NULL, NULL);
            break;
        case btnAddR:
            FrmCustomAlert(myAlert, "Right", NULL, NULL);
            break;
        default:
            break;
    }
    handled = true;
```

A few things to point out about this code structure:

- You will note that it's a switch inside of another switch. This is not unusual for Palm C, so get used to it. The switch is an efficient way of determining various things concerning program operation.

- The first swich refers to a structure **pEvent**, and points to **data.ctlSelect. controlID**. Contained in the pEvent structure is a multi-purpose data section whose contents change according to what kind of event occurred. In this case, because of a control being tapped (marked by **ctlSelectEvent**), the data contained is found under the qualifier **ctlSelect**. If you're really curious about this, please feel free to look up

69

EventType in the Palm Help facility (from the menu bar, choose **Help →
Help Contents**).

- The last statement is, again, our **handled = true** statement.

Step 16. Press **Ctrl+S** to save your changes.

Step 17. On the menu bar, choose **Project → Build All.** Watch the
Console window at the bottom of the screen for the **...done...** compilation
completion message.

Step 18. Start the Garnet OS Simulator and install the Scorer.prc file.
Review the instructions on page 61 if you've forgotten how.

When you start Scorer this time, you'll see the two new text fields and two
new buttons we added. But the magic this time occurs when you tap either of
the "Add L" or "Add R" buttons.

Tapping the "Add L" button produces the screen shown in Figure 29, while
tapping the "Add R" button produces the screen shown in Figure 30.

So now you can see that the buttons work! Hooray!

Figure 30. Tapping "Add L".

Figure 29. Tapping "Add R".

70

You may be wondering why the background for the form is lavender, and the alerts are salmon colored. There's nothing wrong; that is the default color scheme for the Garnet OS Simulator. You can actually go to the Control Panel on the simulator like you would on any Palm device and change the color scheme yourself. But be forewarned – when you close the simulator you'll lose your choices; your selections are not saved.

Best get comfy with lavender and salmon!

Exercise D

For this next exercise, now that we know the buttons work, we're going to add the actual capability of adding one point each time either button is pressed, and to display that on the form. This will get you into working with the field control for the first time.

Don't skip any steps! Everything matters.

Step 1. The first thing we'll need to do is to define two variables that have a global scope – that can be "seen" from inside every function. That matters because more than one function may need access to the variables.

Scroll near the top of the AppMain.c file and in the section labeled "Entry Points", add the following two lines of code:

```
Int16 LScore = 0;          // Left side score
Int16 RScore = 0;          // Right side score
```

These two lines declare two 16-bit signed integers with an initial value of 0.

Step 2. Next, let's create two functions, one for each button, to add one point to a score. Above the function MainFormDoCommand, but under the "Internal Functions" section header, type the following code:

```
void AddLScore(void) {

    FormType* pForm;
    FieldType* pField;
    Char MyStr[10];

    LScore = LScore + 1;
    pForm = FrmGetActiveForm();
    pField = FrmGetObjectPtr(pForm, FrmGetObjectIndex(pForm, txtScoreL));
    StrIToA(MyStr, LScore);
    FldSetTextPtr(pField, MyStr);
    FldDrawField(pField);
}
```

71

```
void AddRScore(void) {

    FormType* pForm;
    FieldType* pField;
    Char MyStr[10];

    RScore = RScore + 1;
    pForm = FrmGetActiveForm();
    pField = FrmGetObjectPtr(pForm, FrmGetObjectIndex(pForm, txtScoreR));
    StrIToA(MyStr, RScore);
    FldSetTextPtr(pField, MyStr);
    FldDrawField(pField);

}
```

At this point, I'm not going to explain the details of what's happening here; just trust me. From Chapter 2, you should recognize some of the names of Palm API functions (the names beginning with "Frm" and "Fld"). Be sure to type carefully.

Step 3. We need to change one little property on the text field controls in order to use the **FldSetTextPtr** function, so double-click on the **AppResources.xrd** node in the **C/C++ Projects** window to open the Palm OS Resource Editor.

Step 4. Click on the text field above the button you labeled "Add L" and look in the Properties section at screen right. Locate the **Editable** checkbox and uncheck it so it's blank. Do the same for the text field above the button you labeled "Add R". Press **Ctrl+S** to save the changes then close the resource editor.

Step 5. Since we have functions to increment the score, they must now be placed where the button events are. Go back to the **MainFormHandleEvent** function and locate the **switch** statement we added after case **ctlSelectEvent**. For the first control – **btnAddL** – add the call to function **AddLScore()** after the first FrmCustomAlert function call. For the second control – **btnAddR** – add the call to function **AddRScore()** after the second FrmCustomAlert function call.

Your code should for the ctlSelectEvent leg should now look like this:

```
case ctlSelectEvent:
    switch (pEvent->data.ctlSelect.controlID) {
        case btnAddL:
            FrmCustomAlert(myAlert, "Left", NULL, NULL);
            AddLScore();
            break;
        case btnAddR:
            FrmCustomAlert(myAlert, "Right", NULL, NULL);
```

```
                AddRScore();
                break;
            default:
                break;
    }
    handled = true;
```

Step 6. Save and compile your program, then start it on the Garnet OS Emulator. After clicking both buttons, you should see the form shown in Figure 31.

But one thing you'll notice right away is that the scores don't change. If you're a truly experienced programmer you know why. Recall that in our function to increment the left side score we have these instructions:

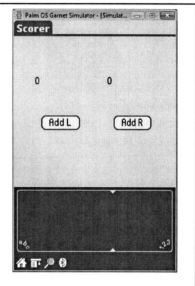

Figure 31. Test Run of Scorer.

```
LScore = LScore + 1;
pForm = FrmGetActiveForm();
pField = FrmGetObjectPtr(pForm,
FrmGetObjectIndex(pForm, txtScoreL));
    FldSetTextPtr(pField, "0");
```

That last statement is what's giving us the problem. We moved a fixed character string "0" to the field pointer represented by the variable pField, rather than taking the value of LScore and converting it to a string for use in that same function call. Let's correct that right now.

Step 7. In the function **AddLScore**, change the line:

```
FldSetTextPtr(pField, "0");
```

to read:

```
StrIToA(MyStr, LScore);
FldSetTextPtr(pField, MyStr);
```

What these two lines do is to take the integer **LScore**, pass it into Palm function **StrIToA**, and convert it to a string. The next line passes the string variable **MyStr** to the text field by way of the pointer variable **pField**.

73

Repeat this step for the function **AddRScore**, using **StrIToA(RScore)**.

Step 8. Since we introduced the new variable MyStr **in both functions**, we now must add a declaration for it, so after the line

```
FieldType* pField;
```

add the line

```
Char MyStr[10];
```

We're going to use "MyStr" as a work string (or holding string), and since its usefulness ends after the string has been displayed, we can actually use it twice.

Step 9. Save the project, recompile it, and install it on the Garnet OS Emulator. Run it and click the "Add L" and "Add R" buttons a few times. In addition to the custom alerts saying "Left" and "Right", you should now also see numbers appearing and increasing by one with each button press. If so, congratulations! You've come quite a ways.

Tired of seeing the custom alerts as you tap the buttons? Then comment them out by placing a "//" before each call to **FrmCustomAlert**.

Need Help?

You can get help using GDS and the Palm API routines by choosing **Help →
Help Contents** on the menu editor. The help facility is searchable by any keyword or function name, so type what confuses you into the search box and click the **Search** button. Any pertinent or associated topics will appear to the left of the screen, and you can choose what you need.

I cover the Help facility in Chapter 17.

Exercise E

For this next exercise, we're going to make a couple of improvements to our Scorer program. We're going to make the numbers larger, and we're going to add places where you can write in the names of the teams or players. This exercise will be simpler than the previous one, because you won't need to write any C routines; it will all be done in the Palm OS Resource Editor. So open your GDS and double-click on the **AppResources.xrd** node to start the resource editor.

74

Step 1. Click on the [+] button in front of **Form**.

Step 2. Double-click on **1000 (Main)** to open the form.

Step 3. Click on the left text field – above the button "Add L" – to select it. You should see the tiny blue dots that indicates it's been selected.

Step 4. In the **Properties** window, locate the property **Font**. Click on the value **"Standard"** and an arrow button will appear. Click on the arrow button and choose **"Large"**.

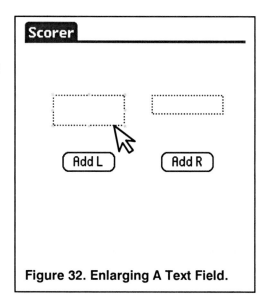

Figure 32. Enlarging A Text Field.

Step 5. Since the font is now larger, we need to make the box larger also. Click on the bottom border of the text field and drag it a little so it's larger (shown in Figure 32).

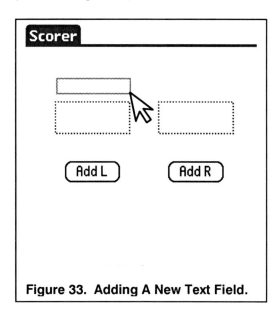

Figure 33. Adding A New Text Field.

Step 6. Repeat Steps 3 through 5 for the text field above the "Add R" button so it's the same size as the left score field.

Step 7. Now we're going to add two new fields in which text can be added. In the **Toolbox**, click on the **Field** button.

Step 8. Above the left text field, click and drag to create a new text field. Make it the same width as the text field underneath it.

Step 9. Repeat Step 8, but for the score field on the right. You should now have two text fields above your larger score fields.

Step 10. Click on the new left text field and in the **Properties** area, locate the **Underlined** property. Double-click on the value **None** and change it to **Gray**.

Step 11. Repeat Step 10 for the text field on the right, changing its **Underlined** property to **Gray**.

If you've followed the steps correctly, you form should now look like the one in Figure 34.

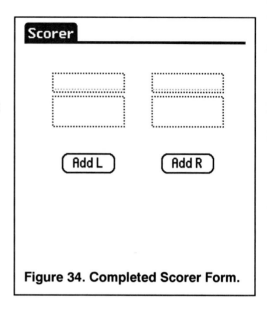

Figure 34. Completed Scorer Form.

Step 12. Save the changes with **Ctrl+S**, then close the resource editor, save the project, and recompile it.

When you start the Garnet OS Simulator, install the program, and run it, now you'll see two dotted lines where you can write in the team or player names. Each press of the buttons underneath adds one point, which is now shown with larger numerals. A sample run of the completed Scorer application (to this point) is shown in Figure 35.

Try It On Your Own Palm Device!

You now have a working Palm application! Sure, it's not very complicated or pretty, but it does work.

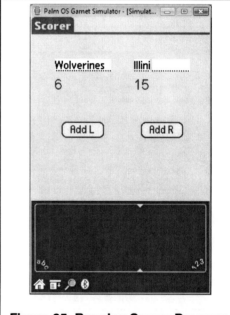

Figure 35. Running Scorer Program.

76

Use the HotSync process to install the Scorer.prc file to your Palm device and run it. It should look exactly like what you've seen on the Garnet OS Simulator.

6.   Saving Information

You may notice that each time you close and reopen the Scorer application, it starts back at 0-0, and the team or player names you typed disappear, meaning you have to rewrite the names and tap the buttons to get back to the scores you had before. We need a way to save the information between uses of the program, and that's the purpose of this chapter – you'll learn how to save information to a **Palm database**.

A Palm database is only a database in the strictest sense of the term – it's a file on a Palm device that holds data. It is not a relational database such as SQL Server or DB2, and it's not even close to that level of sophistication; there is no SQL involved with it. In short, it's not much different than doing random file I-O. The operations you'll be learning in this section essentially allow you to create a file, open it, add records to it, read a record, and close it. That's really all there is to it; everything else you may wish to do with a Palm database is left up to your own creativity and ingenuity.

Before we delve into the next exercise, you might want to go back and briefly review the Data Manager functions from the Palm API back on page 28.

Deeper Waters Ahead!

I'm going to give you a little warning at this point. So far, things have been relatively simple. Database handling is rather a sticky business, so you're about to see a lot of new code that looks like Greek. Type carefully.

Exercise F

If you haven't started the GDS environment, please do so now. The Scorer application – still the only one we've created so far – should open.

Step 1. The first thing we'll need to do is to create a record structure to hold the four pieces of information for this program – namely, the two team names and the two scores. We can accomplish that with the following record structure, which you should type in after your **myAlert** definition in the **Internal Constants** section:

```
typedef struct {                        // Score Data Structure
    Char Name1[21];
    Char Score1[10];
    Char Name2[21];
    Char Score2[10];
} ScorerRec;

ScorerRec ScorerData;                   // Instance of the record
```

We have created four strings – two for the names (Name1, Name2) and two for the scores, represented as strings (Score1, Score2).

Important: In the C language, character strings are always one character shorter in length than allocated. That's because all strings in C must allow one character at the end for a null (hex 00). For the two name variables in the ScorerRec structure above, that means Name1 and Name2 cannot be longer than 20 characters (20 characters plus one null = 21 total). And scores cannot be longer than 9 digits (9 characters plus one null = 10 total).

The record length is the sum of all the lengths of each of the separate variables, so in the case of ScorerRec, the total length will be 62 characters long.

Step 2. We will also need to create a special, global pointer variable to the database. Right after the ScorerRec definition, type the following:

```
DmOpenRef myDB;                         // Pointer to database
```

The **DmOpenRef** data type is a special type for Palm C and is a pointer to a database. DmOpenRef is not a standard C data structure.

We will also need a couple of new, global variables to hold the team names once we retrieve them from the database, so after your declarations for LScore and RScore, add the following lines:

```
Char  LName[21];                        // Left team name
Char  RName[21];                        // Right team name
```

Step 3. Now that we have a record structure to hold the data, we need a function to open the Palm database, and to create one, on-the-spot, if it doesn't exist. Go to the **Internal Functions** section and just after the banner, type the following new function:

```
void OpenDatabase(void) {

    Err myErr;
    MemHandle myHandle;
    UInt16 inx = 0;

    myDB = DmOpenDatabaseByTypeCreator('DATA', 'SCDB', dmModeReadWrite);

    if (!myDB) {

        // Need to create a database now
        myErr = DmCreateDatabase(0, "ScorerData", 'SCDB', 'DATA', false);

        // Open it now that it exists
        myDB = DmOpenDatabaseByTypeCreator('DATA', 'SCDB', dmModeReadWrite);

        // Create a single blank record
        inx = 0;        // choose first record
        myHandle = DmNewRecord(myDB, &inx, sizeof(ScorerData));  // new record
        ScorerPtr = MemHandleLock(myHandle);
        myErr = DmWrite(ScorerPtr, 0, &ScorerData, sizeof(ScorerData));

        StrCopy(ScorerData.Score1, "0");                // set initial display scores
        StrCopy(ScorerData.Score2, "0");

        if (myErr != errNone) {
            FrmCustomAlert(myAlert, "Database write error.", "", "");
        }
        MemPtrUnlock(ScorerPtr);
        DmReleaseRecord(myDB, inx, true);

    } else {

        // It exists; get the names and scores from the database record

        myHandle = DmQueryRecord(myDB, 0);

        ScorerPtr = MemHandleLock(myHandle);                          // move values to
record

        StrCopy(ScorerData.Name1, ScorerPtr->Name1);
        StrCopy(ScorerData.Name2, ScorerPtr->Name2);
        StrCopy(ScorerData.Score1, ScorerPtr->Score1);
        StrCopy(ScorerData.Score2, ScorerPtr->Score2);

        LScore = StrAToI(ScorerData.Score1);                          // convert to
numbers
        RScore = StrAToI(ScorerData.Score2);

        MemPtrUnlock(ScorerPtr);                                      // release
pointer, we have data

    }

}
```

Yes, it's a lot. But try to type carefully. If there's an error, it's probably something you mistyped.

Step 4. Since we have a function to open the database, we also need one to close it. So after OpenDatabase, type the following:

```
void CloseDatabase(void) {

    DmCloseDatabase(myDB);               // Close the database.

}
```

Step 5. We need a function to save the values written into the name fields, so after CloseDatabase, type the following:

```
void SaveFormValues(void) {

    FormType* pForm;
    FieldType* pField;
    Char* myField;                          // Value from text field
    MemHandle myHandle;
    Int16 inx = 0;

    pForm = FrmGetActiveForm();

    // Collect the names

    pField = FrmGetObjectPtr(pForm, FrmGetObjectIndex(pForm, txtNameL));
    myField = FldGetTextPtr(pField);
    StrCopy(ScorerData.Name1, myField);

    pField = FrmGetObjectPtr(pForm, FrmGetObjectIndex(pForm, txtNameR));
    myField = FldGetTextPtr(pField);
    StrCopy(ScorerData.Name2, myField);

    pField = FrmGetObjectPtr(pForm, FrmGetObjectIndex(pForm, txtScoreL));
    myField = FldGetTextPtr(pField);
    StrIToA(ScorerData.Score1, LScore);              // move left score to record

    pField = FrmGetObjectPtr(pForm, FrmGetObjectIndex(pForm, txtScoreR));
    myField = FldGetTextPtr(pField);
    StrIToA(ScorerData.Score2, RScore);              // move rgith score to record


    // Write record to the database

    inx = 0;
    myHandle = DmGetRecord(myDB, inx);  // new record
    ScorerPtr = MemHandleLock(myHandle);
    DmWrite(ScorerPtr, 0, &ScorerData, sizeof(ScorerData));
    MemPtrUnlock(ScorerPtr);
    DmReleaseRecord(myDB, inx, true);

}
```

Step 6. Finally, we need to have a routine to fill the fields on the form. So, type the following function in before OpenDatabase:

```
void FillFormFields(void) {

    FormType* pForm;
    FieldType* pField;
    Char* myField;                          // Value from text field
    MemHandle newHandle;


    pForm = FrmGetActiveForm();


    // Move value from database to first name field

    pField = FrmGetObjectPtr(pForm, FrmGetObjectIndex(pForm, txtNameL));
    myField = FldGetTextPtr(pField);
    newHandle = MemHandleNew(21);                   // choose value equal to fld size
    myField = MemHandleLock(newHandle);             // set handle to string pointer
    StrCopy(myField, ScorerData.Name1);             // copy value to string pointer
    MemHandleUnlock(newHandle);                             // unlock handle
    FldSetText(pField, newHandle, 0, 20);   // move new handle to txt field
    FldDrawField(pField);                                   // refresh so it shows up


    // Move value from database to second name field

    pField = FrmGetObjectPtr(pForm, FrmGetObjectIndex(pForm, txtNameR));
    myField = FldGetTextPtr(pField);
    newHandle = MemHandleNew(21);                   // choose value equal to fld size
    myField = MemHandleLock(newHandle);             // set handle to string pointer
    StrCopy(myField, ScorerData.Name2);             // copy value to string pointer
    MemHandleUnlock(newHandle);                             // unlock handle
    FldSetText(pField, newHandle, 0, 20);   // move new handle to txt field
    FldDrawField(pField);                                   // refresh so it shows up


    // Move value from database to first score

    pField = FrmGetObjectPtr(pForm, FrmGetObjectIndex(pForm, txtScoreL));
    myField = FldGetTextPtr(pField);
    FldSetTextPtr(pField, ScorerData.Score1);
    FldDrawField(pField);                                   // refresh so it shows up


    // Move value from database to second score

    pField = FrmGetObjectPtr(pForm, FrmGetObjectIndex(pForm, txtScoreR));
    myField = FldGetTextPtr(pField);
    FldSetTextPtr(pField, ScorerData.Score2);
    FldDrawField(pField);                                   // refresh so it shows up

}
```

Once you've typed in all this code, save your project, compile it and install it on the Garnet OS Simulator. If you've done it right, your program should like the figures below.

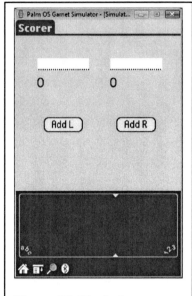

Figure 36. Started.

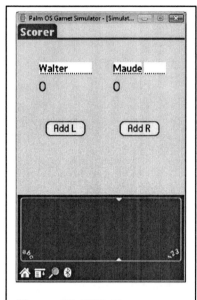

Figure 37. With Names.

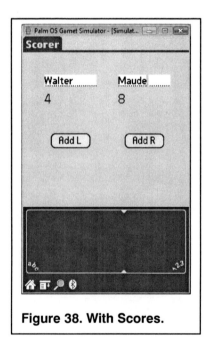

Figure 38. With Scores.

What Did We Just Do??

Wow. You just typed a lot.

And you probably have no idea what you just typed. Not to worry. In this section I'm going to attempt to explain some of what you coded in the previous section.

- At the start of the exercise, we had to define a record structure, because you need a record structure to move data in an out of a Palm database file (a .PDB file that resides on your Palm device).

- We created a database pointer variable – Palm calls it a **DmOpenRef** – to point to the database we're going to access.

- We defined a couple of character strings to serve as work variables – local variables to hold our team or player names.

- We wrote a routine to open the database, conditionally. We check to see if a database exists. If not, we create it on the fly, then we open it. If it does exist, we grab the two names and scores (represented as character strings) from the database file and save those locally.

- We wrote a routine to close the database.

- We wrote a routine to save the values displayed on the form into a record variable, for saving to the database, for when the program exits, so it saves the last scores and team names (so we don't have to start all over again tallying scores).

- And, finally, we wrote a routine to do the converse – to get the values from the database record and to place them on the form, which happens when the program is started and a database is found.

That is what we did!

7. Menus & Dialogs

If you've gotten this far in the book, give yourself a huge pat on the back. You've covered a lot of territory so far.

Now that you have the Scorer application working (I assume you have!) you may have noticed one thing – you can't reset the scores. Each time you tap either of the "Add" buttons, the numbers just keep going up and up. We need to add a way to reset the scores. While I could have required, as the next exercise, adding a third button to reset everything, in this chapter, we're going to add a couple of menu options and have a dialog to confirm the reset.

So, once again, please open your GDS which should still have the Scorer application open.

Exercise G

Step 1. In the **C/C++ Projects** window, double-click on AppResources.xrd to start the **Palm OS Resource Editor**.

Step 2. Under Files, click the [+] button in front of **Menus** (shown in Figure 39). Note that there's a menu resource already defined, **1000 (Main Form)**.

Step 3. Double-click on **1000 (Main Form)**. This will open a work window in which you'll see the menu structure for this application. Right now, there's only one option, **About Scorer**.

Step 4. Click on the node **About Scorer** so it's highlighted.

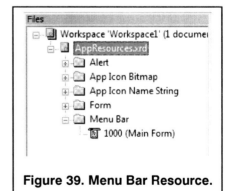

Figure 39. Menu Bar Resource.

Step 5. Right-click on About Scorer and a pop-up menu will appear. Choose the option **Insert Menu Item**. Do it twice, because we're going to add two menu options. Your finished screen should look like Figure 40.

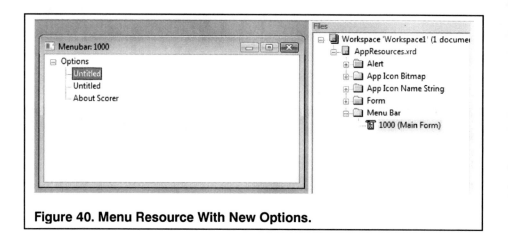

Figure 40. Menu Resource With New Options.

Step 6. Click on the upper "Untitled" node. In the **Properties** window, locate the **Text** property and double-click on the word "Untitled", then overtype it with "Reset Scores". Notice that the Item ID is 1002; we'll be defining a constant for this menu option shortly.

Step 7. Click on the lower "Untitled" node. Again, in the **Properties** window, locate the **Text** property and change the value from "Untitled" to "Clear Names".

TIP: If you want to change the order of the menu items, you can right-click on the item you wish to move, and then choose either **Move Up** or **Move Down**. But be sure to click on the item you want to move (to select it) before moving it up or down in the sequence.

Step 8. Under **Files**, right-click on the **AppResources.xrd** node and a pop-up menu will appear. Choose **New Resource...** and the **New Resource** window appears. We are going to define a new alert, so click on **Alert**. Note that the new alert is assigned the number 1200, which we'll define a constant for shortly.

Step 9. For the **Alert Type** property, change the value from Information to **Confirmation**. You'll see the "i" icon change to a "?".

Step 10. As we did with the custom alert we defined before, we need to change the **Title** property. Under **Properties**, locate Title and change the value to **Confirm Reset**.

Step 11. Under **Properties**, locate **Message** and change the value to "Are you sure you want \nto reset"? What's with the "\n" in there? That's to break the question into two lines. Why break it into two lines? So it fits the box nicely.

Step 12. Finally, we need to add two buttons for "Yes" and "Cancel". In Properties, change **Button 1 Text** from **OK** to **Yes**.

So now you have a single button labeled "OK". But we need a second button. Where is that second button going to come from? Well, a limitation of GDS is that they didn't think of this. However, there is a way we can add the button, but you'll need to change some of the underlying form code to do it. What do I mean? Stick with me.

Step 13. Save your changes and close the Palm OS Resource Editor.

Step 14. In the **C/C++ Projects** window, right-click on the **AppResources.xrd** node. A pop-up menu will appear. Choose **Open With**, which will open a second pop-up menu. Choose the option **Text Editor**. The work area will show code that resembles HTML, as shown:

```xml
<?xml version="1.0" encoding="UTF-8" standalone="yes"?>

<PALMOS_RESOURCE_FILE>

    <ALERT_RESOURCE RESOURCE_ID="1000">
        <ALERT_TYPE> INFORMATION_ALERT </ALERT_TYPE>
        <HELP_ID> 0 </HELP_ID>
        <DEFAULT_BUTTON> 0 </DEFAULT_BUTTON>
        <TITLE> "Scorer Message" </TITLE>
        <MESSAGE> "^1 ^2 ^3" </MESSAGE>
        <BUTTONS>
            <TEXT> "OK" </TEXT>
        </BUTTONS>
    </ALERT_RESOURCE>

    <ALERT_RESOURCE RESOURCE_ID="1100">
        <ALERT_TYPE> CONFIRMATION_ALERT </ALERT_TYPE>
        <HELP_ID> 0 </HELP_ID>
        <DEFAULT_BUTTON> 0 </DEFAULT_BUTTON>
        <TITLE> "Confirm Reset" </TITLE>
        <MESSAGE> "Are you sure you want\nto reset?" </MESSAGE>
        <BUTTONS>
            <TEXT> "Yes" </TEXT>
        </BUTTONS>
    </ALERT_RESOURCE>
```

Every one of the resources is defined with this code, which is called **XML**, or Extensible Markup Language. (You could say HTML is a variant of XML and you'd be right.)

Take a look at the block of code that begins:

```
<ALERT_RESOURCE RESOURCE_ID="1100">
```

because that's what we want to concern ourselves with. The first alert, number 1000, is fine. We just want to add code to the definition for alert number 1100.

Step 15. Skip a few lines down until you find the tag <BUTTONS>. You see there's one line:

```
<TEXT> "Yes" </TEXT>
```

That line represents the Yes button that was already present when we defined the alert. But we need a second one for "Cancel". So make a copy of that line just as you would in Notepad or any other text application: **copy the line, then paste it underneath**. The BUTTONS block of code should look like this (note the lines in bold):

```
<ALERT_RESOURCE RESOURCE_ID="1100">
    <ALERT_TYPE> CONFIRMATION_ALERT </ALERT_TYPE>
    <HELP_ID> 0 </HELP_ID>
    <DEFAULT_BUTTON> 0 </DEFAULT_BUTTON>
    <TITLE> "Confirm Reset" </TITLE>
    <MESSAGE> "Are you sure you want\nto reset?" </MESSAGE>
    <BUTTONS>
        <TEXT> "Yes" </TEXT>
        <TEXT> "Cancel" </TEXT>
    </BUTTONS>
</ALERT_RESOURCE>
```

Step 16. Save the changes by pressing **Ctrl+S**. Close the code file by clicking the "X" button on the tab.

Step 17. Now we need to reset GDS so that it'll open the Palm OS Resource Editor again. In the C/C++ Projects window, right-

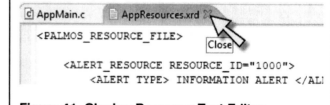

Figure 41. Closing Resource Text Editor.

click on the **AppResources.xrd** node again. For the first pop-up menu that appears, choose **Open With** (as you did before) but on the second pop-up menu that appears, this time, choose **Garnet OS Resource Editor**.

Step 18. Once the resource editor is open, under **Files**, click the [+] button in front of **Alert**. You'll see two alerts, numbered 1000 and 1100. Double-click on Alert 1100, shown in Figure 42.

Take a look at the alert dialog. It has the title you defined, a "?" icon, and two buttons.

Also, take a look in the Properties section. You now see the property **Button 2 Text** in addition to the **Button 1 Text** property that was there originally.

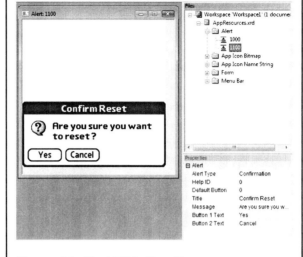

Figure 42. Alert With Two Buttons.

Step 19. We want one more alert, but this one, we want to use to confirm clearing the name text fields. But don't repeat the steps we just went through unless you want to. I'm going to show you a short cut. Right-click on Alert 1100 (shown in Figure 43).

Step 20. Over Alert 1100, right-click to bring up a pop-up menu. This time, choose Paste. You'll see the dialog that's shown in Figure 44. Click the button **Unique ID**. And that's it – you now have a new Alert resource, number 1200, that's the same as the other one.

You can use this same approach to duplicate other resources. This is helpful

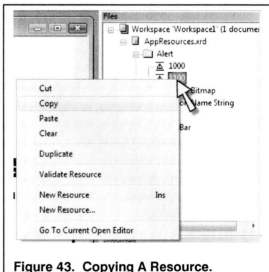

Figure 43. Copying A Resource.

because then you can do all the hard work on creating one resource and then just replicate it.

Step 21. Open Alert 1200 and under **Properties**, change the Title property to "Confirm Clear Names", and the Message property to "Are you sure you want to clear the names?"

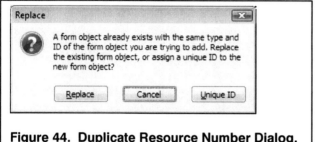

Figure 44. Duplicate Resource Number Dialog.

Step 22. Save your work by pressing **Ctrl+S**.

Step 23. Now we need to define constants for the new controls. In the AppMain.c code window, scroll to the **Internal Constants** section and after your **myAlert** definition, add the following new lines:

```
#define altConfirmReset 1200    // Alert To Clear Scores
#define altConfirmNames 1100    // Alert To Clear Names
#define mnuResetScores  1002    // Menu Option To Reset Scores
#define mnuClearNames   1001    // Menu Option To Clear Names
```

Recall that our new controls have numbers 1100 and 1200. To help distinguish which is which, we've created these new constants.

Step 24. We need to attach the confirmation dialogs to the menu options. First we're going to focus on the Reset Scores. Scroll down to the **MainFormDoCommand** function. Note that the switch statement currently has only one leg, for the value **MainOptionsAboutStarterApp**. If you trace the value of that constant back, you'll see it equals 1000.

We're going to add two new legs.

Step 25. Copy the **case** block of code and paste it twice; there will be three case legs. Change the values for the first two to our new menu constants, **mnuResetScores** and **mnuClearNames**. Then type the following lines:

```
case mnuResetScores:
    reply = FrmAlert(alrtConfirmReset);
    if (reply == 0) {
        ResetScores();
    }
    handled = true;
    break;
case mnuClearNames:
    reply = FrmAlert(alrtConfirmNames);
    if (reply == 0) {
```

```
            ClearNames();
        }
        handled = true;
        break;
```

Step 26. You notice that we have two new functions in that block of code, **ResetScores** and **ClearNames**. Now we need to define both of them. So right above the function **MainFormDoCommand**, add the code for these two functions:

```
void ResetScores(void) {

    FormType* pForm;
    FieldType* pField;
    Char* myField;                          // Value from text field

    LScore = 0;
    RScore = 0;

    pForm = FrmGetActiveForm();

    // Move value from database to first score

    pField = FrmGetObjectPtr(pForm, FrmGetObjectIndex(pForm, txtScoreL));
    myField = FldGetTextPtr(pField);
    FldSetTextPtr(pField, "0");
    FldDrawField(pField);                   // refresh so it shows up

    // Move value from database to second score

    pField = FrmGetObjectPtr(pForm, FrmGetObjectIndex(pForm, txtScoreR));
    myField = FldGetTextPtr(pField);
    FldSetTextPtr(pField, "0");
    FldDrawField(pField);                   // refresh so it shows up

}


void ClearNames(void) {

    FormType* pForm;
    FieldType* pField;
    MemHandle oldHandle;
    MemHandle newHandle;
    Char* myStr;

    pForm = FrmGetActiveForm();

    StrCopy(ScorerData.Name1, "");
    StrCopy(ScorerData.Name2, "");

    // Move blank to first name field

    pField = FrmGetObjectPtr(pForm, FrmGetObjectIndex(pForm, txtNameL));
    oldHandle = FldGetTextHandle(pField);
```

```
newHandle = MemHandleNew(1);                  // choose enough for the field
myStr = MemHandleLock(newHandle);             // critical: must lock handle
StrCopy(myStr, "");
FldSetText(pField, newHandle, 0, 0);
MemHandleUnlock(newHandle);
MemHandleFree(oldHandle);                                  // toss the old handle
FldDrawField(pField);

// Move blank to second name field

pField = FrmGetObjectPtr(pForm, FrmGetObjectIndex(pForm, txtNameR));
oldHandle = FldGetTextHandle(pField);
newHandle = MemHandleNew(1);                  // choose enough for the field
myStr = MemHandleLock(newHandle);             // critical: must lock handle
StrCopy(myStr, "");
FldSetText(pField, newHandle, 0, 0);
MemHandleUnlock(newHandle);
MemHandleFree(oldHandle);                                  // toss the old handle
FldDrawField(pField);

}
```

Closing A Palm Project

Well, that's the end of this particular project. You now have a little pocket scorekeeper you can use for volleyball games, basketball games, or what have you. As an exercise, I invite you to continue to add on to this project using other information in this book.

Right now, I'm going to show you how to close and open projects, because neither is intuitive.

Exercise H

Step 1. In the **C/C++ Projects** window, right-click on the very top node in the tree, the name of the project – in this case, **Scorer**.

Step 2. On the pop-up menu that appears, look for the option **Delete** and select it – circled in Figure 45.

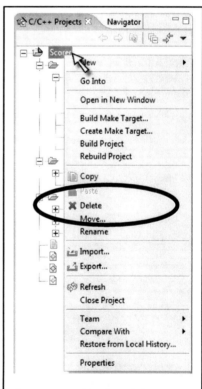

Figure 45. Closing A Project.

Step 3. Here's where you need to be a little careful. A dialog will appear that's titled **Confirm Project Delete**. But there are two radio buttons shown – one that begins, "Also delete contents under …" **DO NOT CHOOSE THAT TOP OPTION.** Click the option underneath it, which should already be chosen: "**Do Not Delete Contents.**" See Figure 46 for an example.

Then underneath, click the **Yes** button (Figure 46) and your entire Palm workspace will clear, just as if you were starting from scratch. **You have not deleted your project**; you've just removed it from GDS. Why the folks that designed GDS didn't come up with a better system than this to close projects, I'm not sure, but remember – GDS is free.

Now, if you ever do wish to delete a project you've worked on, you can choose the upper option "Also delete contents under…", but once you do, your project will be gone for good, so be careful.

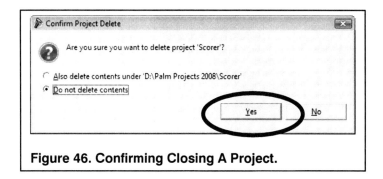

Figure 46. Confirming Closing A Project.

Reopening A Palm Project

All very good and nice, you may be saying to yourself, but how do you reopen a Palm project? The next exercise walks you through reopening our Scorer program.

Exercise 1

Step 1. On the menu bar, choose **File → Import...** as shown in Figure 47.

Step 2. A new window will appear, titled **Import**. Choose the option **Existing Project Into Workspace** if it's not already selected. Then click the **Next** button at the bottom of the window.

Step 3. The next window will let you choose the folder containing the **Project Contents**, so click the **Browse** button. A folder picker window will appear, and you should locate the folder with the name **Scorer** (in this case). Once you've located the folder you want, click **OK** and you're returned to the **Import** window.

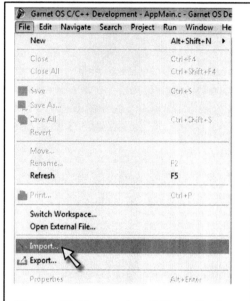

Figure 47. Reopening A Palm Project.

Step 4. Click the **Finish** button. In the **C/C++ Projects** window, you should see the very top of the **Scorer** tree. Click the [+] button in front of the project name **Scorer** and things will open up as before. Remember that to work on the C code, you'll need to click down to the **src** folder and the **AppMain.c** file, and to work on new resources (forms, alerts, buttons, etc.) you'll need to click down to the **rsc** folder and double-click on the **AppResources.xrd** file.

8. Other Controls

In this chapter, we're going to start fresh, with a new project, to let you play with some of the other controls in the resources toolbox. I encourage you to copy the code and routines you find in this chapter into your own projects; reusing code that works is the biggest timesaver you'll ever know with writing for the Palm.

Let's begin!

Exercise J

Open your Garnet OS Development System, if you haven't already. If another project is open, please close it; see Exercise H if you have forgotten how.

Step 1. On the menu bar, choose **File → New → Standard Make 68K C/C++ Project**, as shown in Figure 48.

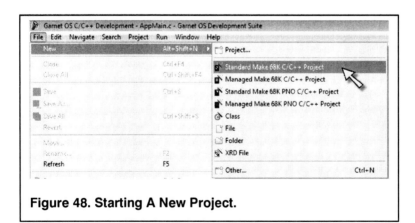

Figure 48. Starting A New Project.

Step 2. When the New Project window appears, type the name **MyDemo** in the **Project name** box, then click the **Next** button.

Step 3. For the **Garnet OS Settings** window, change the Creator ID from STRT to **DEMO**. Do not change any other settings; click the **Next** button.

Step 4. On the Project Code Generation window, click on **Simple Application**. Then click the **Finish** button.

Step 5. After a moment or two, you'll see the blank Palm work area reappear. In the **C/C++ Projects** window, you'll see **MyDemo** at the top of the tree structure. Click the [+] button in front of the name **MyDemo**. Then click the [+] button in front of **rsc**.

Step 6. Double-click on the **AppResources.xrd** node to open the Palm OS Resource Editor.

Step 7. In the Resource Editor, under **Files**, click on the [+] button next to Form. As with all new Palm projects, you'll see two forms already defined for you – **1000 (Main)** and **1100 (About)**. Double-click on **1000 (Main)** to open the form designer.

Step 8. Click on the label "Hello, World!" so it's selected (blue dots around the border) then press the **Delete** key on your computer keyboard.

Step 9. In the **Toolbox**, click on the **Checkbox** button. Then in the form design area, click and drag to place the checkbox control. In **Properties**, change the property from "Untitled" to "Checkbox".

Step 10. Still in the Toolbox, click on the **Field** button. Click and drag on the form to create a field to the right (on the same line) as the checkbox. Under **Properties**, uncheck the **Editable** property.

Step 11. Click on the button **Feedback Slider Con...** which is short for *Feedback Slider Control*. In the form design area, click and drag to place the control in the line underneath the checkbox. Grab one of the blue dots on the right border and shorten the slider so it's about the same length as the checkbox control. Then in the **Properties** window, change the **Maximum** value to 100. **IMPORTANT:** You must have a Minimum value that's less than the Maximum value or your Palm program will not start.

Step 12. Click on the text field on the first line, and on your keyboard press **Ctrl+C** to copy it. Click in a white space somewhere else, then press **Ctrl+V** to paste a copy of it on the form area. It will be pasted on top of the first text field, so you'll need to click and drag this second text field down. Drag it so it's on the same line as the slider.

TIP: To clear the selection of any control on a form, click in any white space on the form.

Step 13. Press **Ctrl+S** to save what you've done so far. Your form should look like the image in Figure 49.

Step 14. Back in the Toolbox, click the **Push Button** button. Then click and drag to create the button on the form. It will have the letter A for the Text property.

Step 15. If the push button is not selected, click on it to select it, then press **Ctrl+C** to copy it. Press **Ctrl+V** to paste a copy of it down on the form and move it to the immediate right of

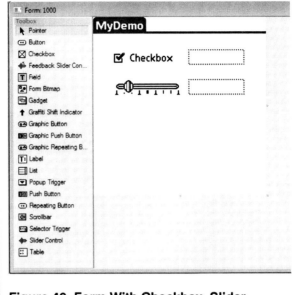

Figure 49. Form With Checkbox, Slider.

the first push button. Change the Text property from A to **B**.

Step 16. Repeat Step 15, but create a box with the letter **C**. Make a copy of the text field control on the second line and drag it to the same line as your three push buttons (A, B, C).

Step 17. In the **Toolbox**, click on the **Pop Up Trigger** button and click and drag a new pop up trigger underneath the push buttons on a fourth line. In the Properties, note there is a List ID that currently has the value 0. We need to define a List. In the Toolbox, there is also a **List** button. Click on that, and click and drag it so it's on top of the Pop Up Trigger. Finally, in the Properties window, uncheck the **Usable** box; this is necessary to tether the list to the trigger.

Step 18. Make a copy of the text field control on the third line and drag it to the same line as the pop up trigger.

After all these steps, your form should look like the one in Figure 50. Right now, nothing does anything, but we're going to fix that in the next exercise.

Press **Ctrl+S** to save your work up to this point.

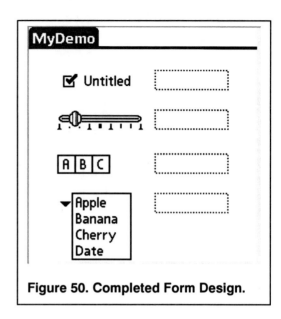

Figure 50. Completed Form Design.

Exercise K

Recall that in the previous exercise, we defined a pop up trigger that requires a list, but we don't have a list yet. We are going to define one now.

Step 1. On the form click on the **List** control – it looks like a blank rectangle. Look in the Properties window to the right of the screen and change the **Num. Items** property from 0 to 4. When you do, you'll see four new properties magically appear – from **Item 0 Text** through **Item 3 Text**.

Step 2. For each of the **Text** properties, type the following values: Apple, Banana, Cherry, Date. Then change the **Num. Vis. Items** property from 0 to 4. You'll see the List box expand in size; you'll be able to see all four of your text values.

Step 3. Look at the top of the **Properties** window for the **ID** – it may be 1010 but note the number that is there.

Step 4. On the form design area, click on the pop up trigger and look at the **List ID** property. If a value has already been assigned, **change it to 0. This is very important.**

What say we compile the program, install it on the Garnet OS Simulator, and run it? It won't do anything, but it'll look cool!

As you play with the program MyDemo, notice that:

- When you click the check box it will go on and off.

- You can slide the slider from left to right.

- You can click on and off each of the A, B and C buttons individually.

But if you click on the pop-up trigger, nothing will happen. That's okay. We're going to add the code to operate that shortly.

Also, recall that we have four unused text fields that are sitting on the form, currently invisible. In the next exercise, you're going to learn how to read each of the controls and send the current value of each control to each text field.

Exercise L

One thing to remember about working with Palm controls is that each of them is associated with a pointer. You'll likely be using the following code segment over and over again:

```
pForm = FrmGetActiveForm();
ctrl = FrmGetObjectPtr(pForm, FrmGetObjectIndex(pForm, ctlSlider));
slide_value = pEvent->data.ctlSelect.value;
```

Where the following are defined in the same function:

```
FormType*      pForm;
ControlType*   ctrl;
```

Once you have the value from **data.ctlSelect.value**, you can do whatever you wish to make it readable, and that will, most likely, mean converting it to a string with the Palm API function **StrIToA**.

We are going to use the code above to interpret the value of each of the four controls and reflect the values in the text fields.

Step 1. With GDS open to the MyDemo project, go to **src** and then to **AppMain.c** and in the Internal Constants section, add the following lines of code:

```
#define chkDemo 1000          // Checkbox
#define fldCheckbox 1001      // Text field for checkbox
```

```
#define sldrDemo 1002        // Slider
#define fldSlider 1003       // Text field for slider
#define pushButtonA 1004     // Push button A
#define pushButtonB 1005     // Push button B
#define pushButtonC 1006     // Push button C
#define fldButtons 1007      // Text field for buttons
#define popupTrigger 1008    // Popup Trigger
#define fldFruits 1009       // Text field for Trigger
#define listFruits 1010      // List for Trigger
```

Be sure to confirm that each of the four-digit numbers shown match those in your form design. If you've added the controls in a different order, the numbering will be different, and should be reflected above.

Step 2. Go to the Palm OS Resource Editor (double-click on **AppResources.xrd**) and define a custom alert with space for three inputs. Create a #define constant **myAlert** equal to 1000.

Step 3. Now let's go to the event handler. Scroll down in the code until you get to the **MainFormHandleEvent** function. The first thing you'll need to do is add some extra variables. Add the following code – typing carefully – after the declaration for pForm:

```
FieldType*     pField;
ControlType*   pControl;
ListType*      pList;
UInt16         ctlValue;
Char           ctlValueStr[10];
Char*          myListChoice;
Int16          listValue;
```

Step 4. Note that there are only two case legs in the switch construct, one for **mnuEvent** and one for **frmOpenEvent**. We are going to a couple of others, to capture changes in controls.

Add the following code to the switch, after the case leg for **frmOpenEvent**:

```
case lstSelectEvent:
    // Normally, I would have a select construct to determine
    // which list was selected but since there's only one, I'll
    // assume it's the only one.
    pForm = FrmGetActiveForm();
    pControl = FrmGetObjectPtr(pForm, FrmGetObjectIndex(pForm, listFruits));

    pList = FrmGetObjectPtr(pForm, FrmGetObjectIndex(pForm, listFruits));

    listValue = pEvent->data.lstSelect.selection;
```

```
            myListChoice = LstGetSelectionText(pList, listValue);
            StrIToA(ctlValueStr, listValue);

            CtlHideControl(pControl);
            CtlSetUsable(pControl, false);

            pControl = FrmGetObjectPtr(pForm, FrmGetObjectIndex(pForm, popupTrigger));

            CtlSetLabel(pControl, myListChoice);     // change the label

            pField = FrmGetObjectPtr(pForm, FrmGetObjectIndex(pForm, fldFruits));

            FldSetTextPtr(pField, myListChoice);
            FldDrawField(pField);            // update the field
            FrmDrawForm(pForm);              // refresh to get update

            handled = true;
            break;

    case ctlSelectEvent:
        // Determine which control changed
        pForm = FrmGetActiveForm();
        switch (pEvent->data.ctlSelect.controlID) {
            case chkDemo:
                pField = FrmGetObjectPtr(pForm, FrmGetObjectIndex(pForm, chkDemo));

                ctlValue = pEvent->data.ctlSelect.on;
                pField = FrmGetObjectPtr(pForm, FrmGetObjectIndex(pForm,
fldCheckbox));
                if (ctlValue == 0) {
                    FldSetTextPtr(pField, "Off");
                } else {
                    FldSetTextPtr(pField, "On");
                }
                FldDrawField(pField);
                break;
            case sldrDemo:
                pField = FrmGetObjectPtr(pForm, FrmGetObjectIndex(pForm,
sldrDemo));
                ctlValue = pEvent->data.ctlSelect.value;
                pField = FrmGetObjectPtr(pForm, FrmGetObjectIndex(pForm,
fldSlider));
                StrIToA(ctlValueStr, ctlValue);
                FldSetTextPtr(pField, ctlValueStr);
                FldDrawField(pField);
                break;
            case pushButtonA:
                pField = FrmGetObjectPtr(pForm, FrmGetObjectIndex(pForm,
fldButtons));
                FldSetTextPtr(pField, "A pressed");
                FldDrawField(pField); // update the field
                FrmDrawForm(pForm);                // refresh to get update
                break;
            case pushButtonB:
                pField = FrmGetObjectPtr(pForm, FrmGetObjectIndex(pForm,
fldButtons));
                FldSetTextPtr(pField, "B pressed");
                FldDrawField(pField); // update the field
                FrmDrawForm(pForm);                // refresh to get update
```

```
              break;
       case pushButtonC:
              pField = FrmGetObjectPtr(pForm, FrmGetObjectIndex(pForm,
fldButtons));

              FldSetTextPtr(pField, "C pressed");
              FldDrawField(pField); // update the field
              FrmDrawForm(pForm);            // refresh to get update
              break;
       case popupTrigger:
              pControl = FrmGetObjectPtr(pForm, FrmGetObjectIndex(pForm,
listFruits));

              CtlShowControl(pControl);
              FrmDrawForm(pForm);            // refresh to get rid of debris
              break;
       }
       handled = true;
       break;
```

Step 5. Once you've added all this code (!), this project is finished. Compile the project, and install it on the Garnet OS Simluator. The completed Palm program, in use, should look like the in Figure 51.

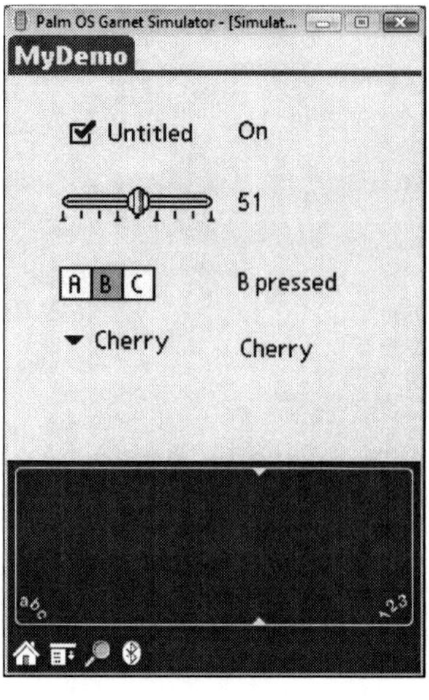

When you click on the check box, the value will change from "On" to "Off".

When you slide the slider bar the value will range between 0 and 100.

When you click one of the buttons, the letter of the last button pressed will show.

When you press the pop-up trigger and make a choice, the choice shows off to the right.

Figure 51. MyDemo.

The code from this program, you can copy into any other Palm projects you do. And that raises a very important point about writing Palm software:

Reuse C Code When Possible

The old saw about reinventing the wheel is just as true when doing Palm software development – learn to reuse your code. Once you sweat getting a particular code sequence to work, why go through the hassles of having to create that code all over again?

As a matter of fact, you may find it helpful, when you're stuck on a particular problem, to search the World Wide Web (the Internet) for code samples, both at ACCESS' web site, as well as other people's blogs or web sites. There are web pages that offer helpful tips and pointers, many more than the scope of this book can hope to cover. That, to a considerable extent, is how I learned to write programs for the Palm.

So be sure to save and backup all your Palm C projects – you never know when they may come in handy in the future!

9. Graphics and Icons

If you're planning on writing a game or another application that uses graphics, you'll need to create the graphics yourself. This chapter is about the creation of graphic objects for Palm projects, including those nifty little blue-dot icons you see on your Palm's main menu area. The main project for this chapter will be a digital clock with large numerals.

Considerations Before Starting A Graphical Project

Before you begin a Palm project that involves graphics, you need to think carefully about a couple of things.

First of all, which classes of Palm devices do you want your project to be able to run on? The original Palm devices had monochrome screens and were 160 x 160 pixels in size, but Palm's latest device, the Centro, has a 320 x 320 screen, and is color. There are very different considerations for both those devices, and the Palm development environment can't make all the decisions for you. Simply put, if you want your program to be able to run on more devices, you'll need to create more graphics up front. But this is not an onerous task, just one for which you'll need to be ready.

Second, you'll need to determine what you want to use to create the graphics. Your graphics will only look as good as (a) your own skill level with creating graphics and (b) the application you use to create them. If you have some experience creating icons for the Windows desktop environment, you're ahead of the game and will have less difficulty. If you've had experience designing games or game sprites, you should also do well.

The Palm OS Resource Editor has facilities for creating graphics built-in, but they're primitive – sufficient for simple tasks only. You may find Windows' built-in program Paint (located in the Accessories folder) to be more user-friendly or other larger applications like Photoshop®, Paint Shop Pro®, Fireworks®, and the like, to give you more control over the creation of your graphics.

Finally, consider the look and feel of your Palm project. What color scheme do you want? Do you want a lot of graphics or just a few?

The Palm Graphics Model

I am going to explain the Palm graphics model in layman's terms, so any of you out there who might think my language simplistic, pardon me – I'm addressing hobbyists rather than geeks.

Let me start describing this model with a screen shot:

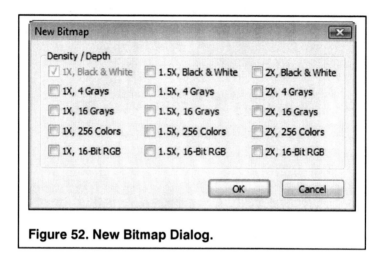

Figure 52. New Bitmap Dialog.

This bewildering collection of fifteen different choices represent all the different ways one bitmap can be represented on the Palm OS platform.

In the left column, everything is at the Palm's normal 160x160 resolution, and ranges from 2-bit color (black & white) all the way up to 16-bit color (16 million colors).

In the middle column, you have the middle resolution, where the maximum is 240x240. It's my impression that this is not in very common use, but it is available.

And in the right column, you have what's called **double density** resolution, or 320x320. Double density is an apt description – bitmap representations are not twice as large, they're twice as "fine", meaning more detail.

Now, when you design graphics for your Palm application, you will have to decide which of these resolutions your application will support. If you're using nothing but Palm's own standard controls, it won't matter, because Palm will automatically do the work of resizing such controls to fit the screen properly.

But if you're doing your own graphics, you'll have to take the different resolutions into account.

As a rule of thumb, you can assume that older Palm devices will use 160x160 resolution. The oldest Palm devices will only operate with 2-bit graphics (black & white). Examples of devices and their supported resolutions are shown in the table below. Generally, devices running Garnet (Palm OS 5) or later will support 320x320 resolution and 16-bit color.

Device	Supported Resolutions
Palm Pilot Personal, Palm Pilot Professional	160x160, black & white
Palm III series	160x160, grayscale
Handspring Visor	160x160, grayscale
Handspring Visor Prism	160x160, 256 colors
Palm Zire 71, Zire 72	320x320, 65,535 colors
Palm Zire 72S	320x320, 65,535 colors
Palm T|X, Centro	320x480, 16 million colors

Table 2. Palm Device Graphic Resolutions.

When you design a bitmap, you'll need to decide how far back you'll want your application to be compatible. For example, if you want to write a color application – such as for a mini video game – you might want to plan on designing your graphics at double density (320x320) using at least 65,535 colors. If you only want your application to run on the very latest Palm devices – such as the new Centro or the T|X – you might only want to design graphics at double density using 16 million colors, the maximum. On the other hand, maybe you want to design a program that runs on everything. In that case, you'll need to design graphics for each of the different resolutions and color depths.

There is no right answer for this; it's all about what you want to do. Think of your target audience and then design accordingly.

Exercise M

For this exercise we're going to design a digital clock with big numerals. It may sound daunting, but it's really not that complicated. We are also going to assume that this clock can run on any Palm device, so you can get an appreciation for evaluating the different bitmap families.

But first, we need to create some graphic numbers!

Step 1. If you have Adobe® Photoshop or a similar graphics program, start it, and create a bitmap of size 40x60. If you don't have an advanced graphics program, then you can start Windows Paint. Paint is in the Accessories folder in Windows. In case you've never seen Paint, check out Figure 53.

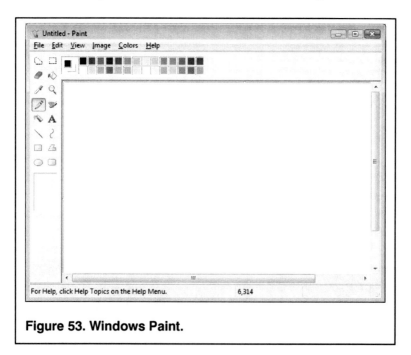

Figure 53. Windows Paint.

Step 2. In order to create number that will fit the Palm screen, we're going to work to a 40x60 grid. So on the menu bar, select **Image → Attributes**.

Step 3. In the **Width** box, type **40** and in the **Height** box, type **60**. Then click OK. The work area will shrink to a small box.

Step 4. Click on the **Text** Tool in the toolbox. The Text tool is marked with a blue "A" icon.

Step 5. Position the crosshatch cursor in the upper left corner of the new image you've created. Click once and a special toolbar appears that lets you choose the font type.

Step 6. Open the first drop-down box and choose **Century Gothic** for the font, and **28** for the size. Click the Bold ("B") button. Do not change the "Western" drop-down box. In the dotted line box, type a zero ("0").

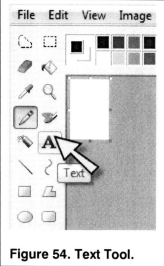

Figure 54. Text Tool.

Step 7. Save the bitmap with the file name **0.bmp**. Note the folder where you save it. Use the **24-bit bitmap** file type.

Step 8. On the menu bar, click **File → New**. This time, you don't have to re-choose the font because you already did that in Step 7. Type a one ("1") in the dotted line box.

Step 9. Save the bitmap with the file name **1.bmp**, again, with the **24-bit bitmap** file type.

Step 10. Repeat Steps 8 and 9 for the numbers 2 through 9, saving to files named **2.bmp** through **9.bmp**. Figure 55 at right shows what you should have.

Figure 55. All Ten Number Bitmaps.

Now, whether you've followed these steps or used your own graphics program, you should now have a set of ten bitmaps representing the numbers from 0 to 9. We now need to import these images into the GDS environment.

If you haven't already opened your GDS environment, please do so now.

Step 11. Close any Palm projects you currently have open, if any.

Step 12. Create a new **Standard 68K C/C++** Project with the name **DClock**.

Step 13. In the **C/C++ Projects** window, double-click on **AppResources.xrd**. This will open the Palm OS Resource Editor.

Step 14. Under **Files**, right-click on the **AppResources.xrd** node in the Files tree. In the pop-up menu that appears, choose **New Resource**.

Step 15. In the **New Resource** dialog that appears, click on Bitmap and then click the **New** button. The bitmap editor will appear with a 1X bitmap at a size of 50x50.

Step 16. The size 50x50 is going to be a little bit large for numbers on a small Palm device, so we're going to change the size to 40x60. We're also going to choose 2X or double density graphics. So in the **Bitmap: 1000** window, click the **Delete** button. You will see a warning message like the one shown in Figure 56 below. Click **Yes** to this.

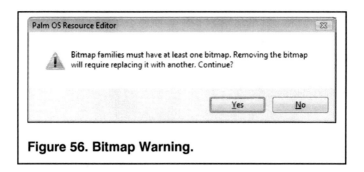

Figure 56. Bitmap Warning.

Step 17. This dialog will be replaced by the same dialog you saw in Figure 52, showing all the different graphics modes. You will note that the **1X Black & White** choice is grayed out, because we just deleted it.

Click on the **2X, 16-Bit RGB** checkbox then click **OK**. Now, your design window should look like the one in Figure 57:

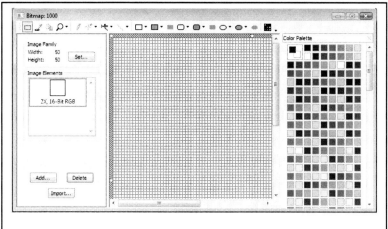

Figure 57. Bitmap Design Window, In 2X Mode.

Step 18. We are now going to import, one at a time, each of the number bitmaps we created in the first half of this exercise. Click the button **Import...** near the lower left corner of the design window. It's next to the **Add...** button. Once you click the **Import** button, the **Open** dialog window appears, shown below in Figure 58. Point to the folder that contains your number bitmaps, and choose the first in the series, the file **0.bmp**.

Click the **Open** button to complete your selection.

Step 19. Next, you'll see a warning message indicating the size of the bitmap we created – 40x60 – is not the same as the default size – 100x100. Anytime bitmaps don't match you will see this

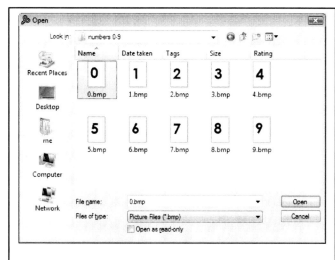

Figure 58. Selecting A Bitmap To Import.

warning (Figure 59), so get used to it. There will always be four options (one of which may be grayed out). Generally speaking, you have the choice of truncating the new image or shrinking the new image proportionally.

Choose **Scale existing images to new image size**, shown in Figure 59 at right. Once you've made this choice and clicked OK, the bitmap you created will show up in the design area. You will also notice that the Width and Height fields change to 20 and 30. Why is this? Remember that we're creating an image for **double density**. Our original bitmap pattern was 40x60 so the "base" (or 1X) bitmap will be 20x30. **Click Ctrl+S to save your bitmap.**

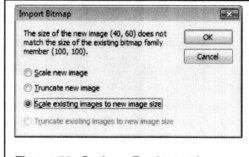

Import Bitmap

The size of the new image (40, 60) does not match the size of the existing bitmap family member (100, 100).

OK
Cancel

○ Scale new image
○ Truncate new image
◉ Scale existing images to new image size
○ Truncate existing images to new image size

Figure 59. Options For Importing.

You will also notice something else interesting, something you may not have noticed when looking up close at a bitmap before. Your all-black number is not all black! If you look at the left and right edges of the number 0, you'll see some shades of brown and blue. This is a graphic "trick" called **anti-aliasing**, and it's been around almost since the beginning of Microsoft Windows. Anti-aliasing uses a variety of colors to fool the eye into thinking it's seeing a smooth line rather than the jagged sort of bitmaps you see at lower bit densities. But you will likely only see anti-aliased text like this at higher bit densities – such as for 2X, 16-bit RGB color.

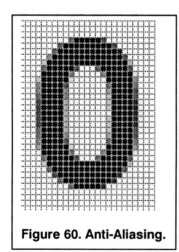

Figure 60. Anti-Aliasing.

You'll really only notice anti-aliasing in the design phase, such as when you import a bitmap. Only more sophisticated Palm users can tell the difference between a bitmap that's anti-aliased and one that isn't. Such users will say that one bitmap looks smooth and the other has "the jaggies".

Anti-aliased text is not possible on the earliest versions of the Palm operating system, so keep this in mind when designing your bitmaps.

Let's take a look at your design window at the moment, shown in Figure 61 below:

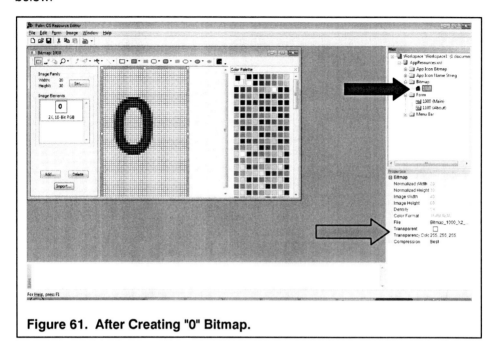

Figure 61. After Creating "0" Bitmap.

You can see that:

- In the **Files** tree, there's a node 1000 representing the "0" bitmap in the main work area (marked by the top arrow in Figure 61). At the moment it is the only bitmap. The number **1000** is the control ID number.

- The **Properties** window has a number of traits associated with this bitmap, many of which are in gray. You will not be changing any of the numbers in gray. But notice the Transparent and Transparency Color properties (marked by the bottom arrow). If you ever design a game and you want to create a sprite, you will change these properties so that the bitmap can show on a game background using whatever background color you choose. The background color is currently white (R=255, G=255, B=255), but that's okay because our numbers will not be transparent.

Now we need to create bitmaps for the numbers 1 through 9.

Step 20. Repeat Steps 15 through 19 to create new bitmap resources, and import bitmap images. The new bitmaps will be numbered **1100** for "1", **1200** for "2", **1300** for "3", and so forth until reaching **1900** for "9". You will have a total of 10 bitmaps.

If you've done this correctly, your Palm OS Resource Editor should look something like the one in Figure 62.

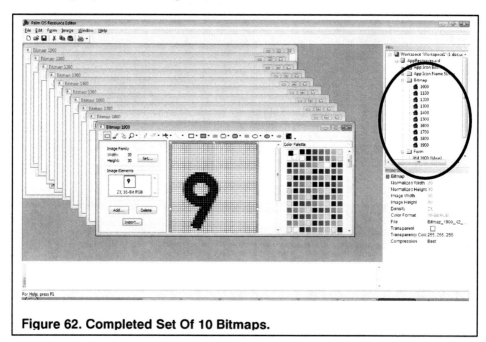

Figure 62. Completed Set Of 10 Bitmaps.

Note that each of the bitmaps numbered 1000 to 1900 appear in the **Files** tree under "Bitmap" (circled in red above).

Step 21. Close the Palm OS Resource Editor. We don't need to do anything else with the bitmaps at this point. In the next exercise we're going to focus on the logic to make the bitmaps appear on the Palm screen, and determine how to change the system's built-in clock into a set of six bitmaps that display the time.

Exercise N

This exercise is a continuation of Exercise M, so if you haven't already done the steps in Exercise M to create a set of 10 number bitmaps, please go back and do that first.

Before we go a step further, I'm going to list a few things that the logic part of this Palm program, our digital clock, will have to do. It will need to:

- Read the current time from the system clock

- Convert the time to a character string

- Convert each digit in the character string, one by one, into a bitmap and place the bitmap from left to right according to which digit is being written.

- Have a mechanism for updating the time on the display every second

Sounds reasonable, right? Let's get down to it.

Please start your GDS environment and open the DClock project if you haven't already got it open.

Step 1. Open **AppMain.c** and scroll down to near the end of the code, looking for the **AppEventLoop** function. Change this line:

```
EvtGetEvent(&event, evtWaitForever);
```

to this:

```
EvtGetEvent(&event, 100);
```

What this does is to change the main event loop from waiting indefinitely to waiting every one second – or 100 ticks. On your Palm device, 100 ticks probably equals one second.

Step 2. Near the end of the do-loop, locate this line:

```
FrmDispatchEvent(&event);
```

and add this line right above it:

```
PrintTime();
```

This is a call to a function that we haven't yet defined, but based on the name, you can see what it will do – it will print out the time on the display.

Step 3. Go to the top of the code and after the Internal Constants banner, add the following code after the definition for **appDevVersionNum**:

```
#define myAlert 1000
#define fldTime 1000
Int16 timex;
Int16 timey;
```

You can see the first two statements define constants for a custom alert and for a test field for the time. The next two are 16-bit integers used to display the bitmaps.

Step 4. Go to the top of the code and after the Internal Functions banner:

```
/**********************************************************************
 *
 *   Internal Functions
 *
 **********************************************************************/
```

type the following new functions:

```
void MyDrawBitmap(UInt16 resID, Coord x, Coord y)
{
    MemHandle resH;
    BitmapPtr resP;

    resP = NULL;
    resH = DmGetResource(bitmapRsc, resID);

    ErrFatalDisplayIf(!resH, "Missing bitmap");
    resP = (BitmapPtr)MemHandleLock(resH);

    WinDrawBitmap(resP, x, y);
    MemPtrUnlock(resP);
    DmReleaseResource(resH);
}

void PrintTime(void) {

    UInt32 Elapsed;
    DateTimeType Now;
    Char NowStr[20];
    Char n[5];                      // work string for a number
    FormType*    pForm;
    FieldType*  pField;
    Char Curr;
    Int16 p;
```

```
timex = 1;
timey = 70;

Elapsed = TimGetSeconds();
StrIToA(NowStr, Elapsed);

TimSecondsToDateTime(Elapsed, &Now);

StrCopy(NowStr, "");                    // reset the string

StrIToA(n, Now.hour);
if (Now.hour < 10)
    StrCat(NowStr, "0");                // add leading zero if < 10
StrCat(NowStr, n);

StrIToA(n, Now.minute);
if (Now.minute < 10)
    StrCat(NowStr, "0");                // add leading zero if < 10
StrCat(NowStr, n);

StrIToA(n, Now.second);
if (Now.second < 10)
    StrCat(NowStr, "0");                // add leading zero if < 10
StrCat(NowStr, n);

pForm = FrmGetActiveForm();
if (pForm != NULL) {
    pField = FrmGetObjectPtr(pForm, FrmGetObjectIndex(pForm, fldTime));
    FldSetTextPtr(pField, NowStr);
    FrmDrawForm(pForm);
}

for (p = 0; p < 6; p++) {

    Curr = NowStr[p];

    switch(Curr) {
        case '0': MyDrawBitmap(1000, timex, timey); break;
        case '1': MyDrawBitmap(1100, timex, timey); break;
        case '2': MyDrawBitmap(1200, timex, timey); break;
        case '3': MyDrawBitmap(1300, timex, timey); break;
        case '4': MyDrawBitmap(1400, timex, timey); break;
        case '5': MyDrawBitmap(1500, timex, timey); break;
        case '6': MyDrawBitmap(1600, timex, timey); break;
        case '7': MyDrawBitmap(1700, timex, timey); break;
        case '8': MyDrawBitmap(1800, timex, timey); break;
        case '9': MyDrawBitmap(1900, timex, timey); break;
    }

    timex = timex + 20;

}

}
```

Now let me attempt to explain what these two functions are, and why we need them.

The first function, **MyDrawBitmap**, is quite simple – it simplifies the process of displaying a bitmap. There are many variations of this routine on the World Wide Web, but most of them look about the same as this one. The Palm API can do many things, but unfortunately for the end user, not all of them are easily accomplished or intuitive. You might find other elementary processes such as this one, displaying a bitmap at a given x, y coordinate, from which you can create your own functions.

The second function, **PrintTime**, is a little more elaborate. What PrintTime does is to display the time as a series of six bitmaps (one for each numeral in a 24-hour clock display with positions for hours, minutes and seconds).

These two statements…

```
timex = 1;
timey = 70;
```

…set the starting values for where the bitmaps will be written. This clock will start at position (1,70).

NOTE: Even though point placements are expressed using the 1X coordinate system, when you use double density (2X) graphics, you must still place them on the screen using 1X coordinates. If that sounds wrong to you, remember that double density graphics means twice the graphical *density*, NOT twice the size.

What will happen – and I'm risking getting ahead of myself here – is that each time a bitmap is painted to the form, we will increment the **timex** variable by the width of the number bitmap – in this case, 20 pixels. The timey variable will remain unchanged, placing the time display roughly vertically centered on the screen.

Then we come to these lines:

```
Elapsed = TimGetSeconds();
StrIToA(NowStr, Elapsed);
```

The first line calls the no-argument Palm API function **TimGetSeconds**, which returns the number of seconds since January 1, 1904 at 0:00 hours (midnight). Since that's a relatively useless quantity in and of itself, we will be converting that to a series of data including an hour, minute, and second.

The **StrIToA** function converts the variable Elapsed to a character string NowStr. I did this to have a way of double-checking that you are getting the time, should you decide to use a custom alert right then and there (it is cleared out a few lines down; I don't mind reusing variables and you shouldn't, either). The variable NowStr isn't really necessary in this program otherwise.

Next, we come to this line:

```
TimSecondsToDateTime(Elapsed, &Now);
```

Veterans of C programming will recognize that the second argument to this Palm API function is the *address* of the variable Now; the function **TimSecondsToDateTime** expects an integer first and a pointer to a DateTime variable second. This function takes a 32-bit unsigned integer and converts it to an internal record structure represented by **DateTimeType**, which contains an hour, a minute, and a second. It also has date information but we don't currently care about that.

TIP: Feel free to use the **Palm API Built-In Help Facility**; I have found it to be quite helpful. Looking up functions and data structures will help you understand the way Palm designers were thinking (for better or worse). You can find this treasure trove of information on the menu bar under **Help → Help Contents**.

After our time function call, you see a set of three code blocks that look similar to this:

```
StrIToA(n, Now.hour);
if (Now.hour < 10)
    StrCat(NowStr, "0");          // add leading zero if < 10
StrCat(NowStr, n);
```

Now is a record type of DateTimeType, containing the three integer variables (or fields) **hour**, **minute** and **second**. For the design of this program I wanted the time to always be represented as a 6-character string without colons – that is, *HHMMSS*. Values less than 10 are left-padded with a leading zero.

This block of code (a) converts the hour to a character string n, (b) checks to see if the hour is less than 10 and if so, (c) prepends a "0" to the time string, and finally (d) adds the string representation of the hour.

If, for example, the hour of the day is 8 a.m., then **Now.hour** will be equal to the value 8, and after this first swipe of code, **NowStr** will equal "08".

This block of code is repeated for the minute and second. Note that the character string NowStr is built upon using the Palm API function **StrCat**, which is a right-sided concatenation function – that is, new substrings are added to the *right* side of an existing string. (For some mysterious reason, Palm did not include a left-sided concatenation function. Guess they have something against Southpaws.)

Next, we have code to obtain the pointers to the form and that debug text field:

```
pForm = FrmGetActiveForm();
if (pForm != NULL) {
    pField = FrmGetObjectPtr(pForm, FrmGetObjectIndex(pForm,
fldTime));
    FldSetTextPtr(pField, NowStr);
    FrmDrawForm(pForm);
}
```

The Palm API function **FrmGetActiveForm** is handy to use any time you plan on doing a form operation; you can't really go wrong using it, because it spares you having to maintain a pointer to the form.

The if/then block of code that follows ensures that a pointer exists – that is, that a form is actually there (things move quickly in the Palm environment and the first time this function is called, there may not be anything there yet, believe it or not), and if it finds one, gets a pointer to the text field and writes out our 6-character string representing the time, perhaps something like "093452" or (if you're a night owl like me) "235937" for 11:59:37pm. That 6-character string NowStr is written to the form using the **FldSetTextPtr** function, and the entire form is refreshed with a call to **FrmDrawForm**.

IMPORTANT: If you change the appearance of a text field, button, etc., please remember to call **FrmDrawForm** to repaint changes, otherwise you might see some "garbage" characters when you run your application.

At the end of this function is a rather involved for-loop, which I show at the top of the next page.

```
for (p = 0; p < 6; p++) {

    Curr = NowStr[p];

    switch(Curr) {
        case '0': MyDrawBitmap(1000, timex, timey); break;
        case '1': MyDrawBitmap(1100, timex, timey); break;
        case '2': MyDrawBitmap(1200, timex, timey); break;
        case '3': MyDrawBitmap(1300, timex, timey); break;
        case '4': MyDrawBitmap(1400, timex, timey); break;
        case '5': MyDrawBitmap(1500, timex, timey); break;
        case '6': MyDrawBitmap(1600, timex, timey); break;
        case '7': MyDrawBitmap(1700, timex, timey); break;
        case '8': MyDrawBitmap(1800, timex, timey); break;
        case '9': MyDrawBitmap(1900, timex, timey); break;
    }

    timex = timex + 20;

}
```

The "Toteboard Engine"

Seasoned programmers can probably guess what's going on above, but I'm going to explain it anyway. This little cluster of code is what I like to call a **"toteboard engine"**. A toteboard engine is a block of code – or a function – that has as its sole purpose the graphical display of a string of characters using bitmaps – that is, with numerical characters on a toteboard or clock, or alphabetical characters in, for example, a word game or language translator program.

A toteboard engine can be summarized this way:

For each character in the input string, determine which character is the current character and paint a bitmap in the next available position on the toteboard-style display. Proceed until all the characters in the input string have been exhausted (or the display is out of space).

That, in essence, is all there is to it. Note that the Curr assignment looks at one character at a time in the time string (e.g., "153029"), runs it through the 10 consecutive **case** legs, and when it finds the right numeral, calls the MyDrawBitmap function with the **resource ID** (the 4-digit number), and the **timex** and **timey** placement variables. Once a bitmap has been painted on the

123

display, the value of **timex** is incremented by the width of the bitmap (at single density).

Now, the really industrious souls among you could simply replace the **switch** construct with some kind of function to determsine the resource ID programmatically – after all, it is a 4-digit integer:

```
MyDrawBitmap((1000 + n*100), timex, timey); break;
```

But if you ever get messed up in the bitmap definition process, and the numbering gets screwed up, you might find using a switch construct to be a little more straightforward. Spelling out all the case legs is essential if you plan on using **#define** statements to create constants for each of your bitmaps (which, by the way, you do not *have* to do; it is a good practice, though). Also, do remember that with **case** legs, each can only represent a **single character** – hence the single quotation marks; you cannot use double-quotes, and you cannot use strings of 2 characters or longer in case legs or a parse error (syntax error) will result.

Step 5. That is all there is to this program, so save your work, compile it, and install it on the Garnet OS Emulator. If you've succeeded, your program will look something like Figure 63. If you were smart enough to remove the "Hello, World!" label, gold star for you!

Now, why aren't there any colons in the display? We did not define any colon bitmaps, that's why. As another exercise, you might try defining a colon bitmap and figure out how to place it.

Or, you might try centering the six digits. I'll give you a hint: it involves changing the starting value of the **timex** variable.

If you really feel like making your clock stylish, create multicolored numbers. Just remember that each number you create, you'll need to import to the Palm OS Resource Editor. But then your clock will look more interesting and have your stamp of originality on it!

Figure 63. DClock, Running.

Another Way To Get Text On A Form

You may recall that you can put text on a form with either a label control (like the "Hello, World!" label in the base Palm application) or with a text field. But for those two methods, the text will always be black. What if you want to "paint" text in red, such as for a warning message, or in green, to indicate an action completed successfully?

Fortunately, the set of Palm API functions includes a set of functions oddly named "Windows" functions. They, of course, have nothing to do with Microsoft Corporation and how they got that name is beyond me. But the thing to realize is all such API functions start with "Win" in their names, and the one we're most interested in for the purpose of painting text on a form is **WinPaintChars**.

For example, suppose you wanted to paint the words "CLICK TO BEGIN" in red. First, you would need to define an **RGBColorType**, a pointer to a color. For pure red, you could add this to the top of one of your own functions:

```
RGBColorType  pure_red;
pure_red.r = 255;
pure_red.g = 0;
pure_red.b = 0;
```

Next, you would set the color of text to this color by calling the **WinSetTextColorRGB** function, like so:

```
WinSetTextColorRGB(&pure_red, NULL);    // must add the '&'!!!
```

Then, you would tell processing to write the text without any background color by using the **WinSetDrawMode** function:

```
WinSetDrawMode(winOverlay);              // transparent
```

Finally, you would actually print your text out by using the **WinPaintChars** function, like this:

```
WinPaintChars("CLICK TO BEGIN", StrLen("CLICK TO BEGIN"), 20, 40);
```

Note that this API function call not only requires you to pass in the string or string variable for the first parameter, you **must** also pass in the **length of the string or string variable** in the second parameter. The last two parameters are the x and y coordinates for where the string will be printed out; in this case, "CLICK TO BEGIN" will print at (20, 40) on the form.

It would be wise of you to define an RGBColorType for black (or whatever default text color you'd need) and making it a global variable, thus:

```
RGBColorType* basic_black;
basic_black->r = 0;
basic_black->g = 0;
basic_black->b = 0;
```

And for white, of course, you could define it as such:

```
RGBColorType* snow_white;
snow_white->r = 255;
snow_white->g = 255;
snow_white->b = 255;
```

Having such colors and the ability to paint them anywhere, even overlaying existing bitmaps you may have painted with earlier instructions in a function, gives more flexibility to how you can define the look of a program.

Erasing Text

So how would you erase text you painted on a form? You can do it by using the **WinSetTextColorRGB** function to set the text color to the same color as the background and calling **WinPaintChars** with the same parameters you used previously.

Another, more slightly creative approach would be to pre-define a bitmap as a Palm resource and calling the user-defined MyDrawBitmap function (see page 117) to overlay the text. If you know the length of your longest text string, this gives the advantage of letting you "reset" your text area by painting with the same bitmap over and over. You might find such an approach suitable if you have to have text that changes dynamically, such as painting a time of day clock in a lower corner of the form, or updating a score for a game.

Always remember to use the **FrmDrawForm** function to refresh the form after calling painting functions.

Other Graphics Functions

Here's a short list of other graphics functions you may wish to try on your own, documented in the Palm API Documentation (the Help facility). Each of them paints "programmatically", meaning if you want to pass variables to the functions to accomplish the rendering of graphics, you may do so.

- **WinPaintLine.** Paints a line on the form from one (x,y) coordinate to another. Uses the last set paint foreground color.

- **WinPaintPixel.** Paints a single pixel on the form.

- **WinPaintRectangle.** Paints a rectangle on the form. Requires you to define a pointer variable to a RectangleType variable. Also lets you specify the roundness of the corners if you want a rounded rectangle.

And, in order to set colors you will need these API functions:

- **WinSetBackColorRGB.** Sets the background color for subsequent painting operations; does not instantaneously change the background color of the form. Requires you to pre-define a color as an RGBColorType pointer variable. RGBColorType is a record structure with individual values "r" (red value, 0 to 255), "g" (green value, 0 to 255), and "b" (blue value, 0 to 255).

- **WinSetForeColorRGB.** Sets the foreground color for subsequent painting operations, **not** including text (see WinSetTextColorRGB for that). As with WinSetBackColorRGB, this function requires you to pass in an RGBColorType pointer variable.

- **WinSetTextColorRGB.** Sets the text color for subsequent painting operations. To be used in conjunction with **WinPaintChars**.

- **WinSetUnderlineMode.** Sets text to underline mode for subsequent painting operations. To be used in conjunction with **WinPaintChars**.

Check the Palm API for the calling parameters for each of these functions.

There are other "Win" graphics functions besides the ones listed here, which I will leave to you as an exercise to look up in the Palm API Documentation.

10. Multiple Bitmap Families

Back in Chapter 3, I very briefly mentioned that one thing you'd have to do differently that you couldn't take for granted was being able to design one set of bitmaps for an application and being done with it. With the Palm platform, because there are different classes of devices – although the older ones are becoming less used as newer ones replace them – you may wish to be sensitive to Palm device owners with lesser graphics capabilities.

This means that instead of just one set of bitmaps for an application, you may need two or three. If you want maximum graphic compatibility going back to the earliest Palm devices, you'll need three, four, or more.

The latest Palm devices – such as the new (as of this publication) Centro – run the Garnet OS (formerly known as Palm OS 5) and use 16-bit color on a 320x320 screen.

Palm devices that support higher color depth graphics are also able to do anti-aliasing (as mentioned in the previous chapter), while those devices limited to 2-bit graphics (black & white) cannot, meaning some graphics won't just look more jagged in appearance; in some cases you won't be able to tell what's in the image.

This chapter includes an exercise that will show you how one bitmap will look when imported to the Palm OS Resource Editor at different color depths. You will need to make the call on whether it will be worth your time to develop your application for different devices.

Palm's Basic Controls Not Affected

Thankfully, these considerations do not extend to Palm's collection of controls. Buttons, checkboxes, labels, text fields, and the rest are automatically adjusted graphically depending on the device on which they're running. What that means is that if you've designed a Palm application, the buttons and text will be rendered at double density on high-end devices such as the Centro or T|X, but at lower, single density on lower-end devices such as the Palm III or Handspring Visor.

Exercise O

Step 1. Locate a color image. This can be a photograph, a logo, or something similar, but be sure it has lots of colors. A photograph would be ideal for this exercise because most photos contain millions of color gradations. If the image is in a file that does not have an extension of BMP, be sure to convert the file to a BMP (or bitmap). Most high-end graphics applications like Photoshop and Paint Shop Pro have such facilities built in. Resize the image down to a maximum of **160 x 160 pixels**.

Step 2. Start the Garnet OS Development System, close any projects that you may have opened, and create a new **Standard 68K C/C++ Project** with the name **ColorTst**.

Step 3. In the **C/C++ Projects** window, expand the ColorTst tree. Expand the **rsc** node until you see **AppResources.xrd**. This starts the Palm OS Resource Editor.

Step 4. Under Files, double-click on the **Form** node, then double-click on **1000 (Main)** to open the form designer.

Step 5. Click on the "Hello, World!" label and press the **Delete** button on your keyboard to delete it.

Step 6. Under **Files**, click on the **AppResources.xrd** node in the tree to select it. Right-click on this node and on the pop-up menu that appears, choose **New Resource**.

Step 7. On the **New Resource** window, click **Bitmap**, and then the **New** button. You will now see a workspace window with the title bar "**Bitmap: 1000**".

Before we continue, I'd like to show you the bitmap I chose to demonstrate this exercise. To the right you see a photograph I took of a cluster of colored ribbons (trust me, the original was color). I reduced the photo to 140 x 140 (to allow a small white border). This photo will demonstrate just how different the various color depths are.

Step 8. Note that in the Image Elements box, it reads "1X, Black and White". This is the lowest resolution possible for any Palm device. A bitmap at this resolution will run on every device from the first PalmPilot to the latest Palm device or Treo smartphone.

Click the **Import** button, shown in Figure 64.

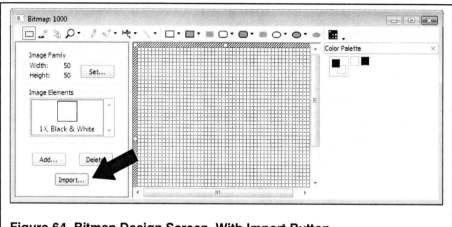

Figure 64. Bitmap Design Screen, With Import Button.

Step 9. Locate the folder containing the image you want to import and select the file with your bitmap image. If your image is not 50 x 50 pixels (the default size), you will receive a warning message asking what you want to do. Choose **Scale existing images to new image size**.

Step 10. Maximize the **Bitmap:1000** window and take a look at what's present. If you did it correctly, you should see a rather ugly black and white set of splotches. That is what happens when a 16-bit image is reduced to monochrome color density. While this image could be supported by an early generation Palm device, it looks awful. The lesson: black & white should only be used for illustrations you've created pixel-by-pixel, not for imported graphics or photographs.

Figure 65. Monochrome Bitmap.

Step 11. Now we're going to add another bitmap color depth. Click the Add button and on the **New Bitmap** dialog that appears, choose "**1X, 4 Grays**". Then click on OK. What we're doing here is to create a second bitmap family. Note that the Image Elements box now has two bitmap families checked: *1X, Black & White*, and *1X, 4 Grays*.

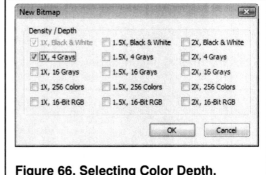

Figure 66. Selecting Color Depth.

Step 12. Click the **Import** button and locate the same folder as before, with the same bitmap image as before.

Step 13. Maximize the **Bitmap:1000** design window and take a look. Not much better, is it? This bit depth was used on some early Palm devices.

One important thing to realize about Palm devices is that **they will use the highest bit depth defined**. This is why you need multiple bitmap families, and should **try to define as many as practicable**. If a Palm device doesn't find a family defined for a color depth it expects, it won't render anything, meaning the application will show a blank space where a bitmap is supposed to be.

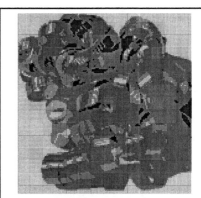

Figure 67. Bitmap: 1X, 4 Grays.

Step 14. Now we're going to add another bitmap color depth. Click the Add button and on the **New Bitmap** dialog that appears, choose "**1X, 16 Grays**". Then click on OK. Note that the Image Elements box now shows three bitmap families checked: *1X, Black & White*, and *1X, 4 Grays*, and *1X, 16 Grays*.

Step 15. Maximize the **Bitmap:1000** design window and look again. The image is becoming more recognizable.

With this latest import, at least you can now see the images (at right) are ribbons. But there's still no color. Your image probably looks no better.

Let's move into the color spectrum (which, regrettably, won't show in color in this book).

Step 14. Let's add another bitmap color depth. Click the Add button and on the **New Bitmap** dialog that appears, choose "**1X, 256 Colors**". Then click on **OK**. Note that the Image

Figure 68. Bitmap: 1X, 16 Grays.

Elements box now shows four bitmap families checked: *1X, Black & White*, and *1X, 4 Grays*, *1X, 16 Grays*, and *1X, 256 Colors*.

Step 15. Click the **Import** button and locate the same folder as before, with the same bitmap image as before.

Step 16. Maximize the **Bitmap:1000** design window and look again. Now we have color, albeit a bit simplistic looking. It's closer to a photo, but it looks a bit posterized.

Figure 69. Bitmap: 1X, 256 Colors.

If you're writing an applications with simple graphics, this color depth would probably be suitable for you. This would run reasonably well on the first generation of Palm devices such as the Visor Prism. But it would be running well below the graphic capability of better devices such as the current Z22, the Zire 72, or the Palm Centro.

Now we're going to go for the maximum bit depth.

Step 17. Let's add one more bitmap color depth. Click the **Add** button and on the **New Bitmap** dialog that appears, choose "**1X, 16-Bit RGB**". Then click on OK. The Image Elements box now shows five bitmap families checked: *1X, Black & White*, and *1X, 4 Grays*, *1X, 16 Grays*, *1X, 256 Colors*, and our last one, *1X, 16-Bit RGB*.

Step 18. Click the **Import** button and locate the same folder as before, with the same bitmap image as before.

Step 19. Maximize the **Bitmap:1000** design window and look again. Finally (in this case) we have something that resembles a photograph. Something at this bit depth would look great on the highest-level Palm devices, such as the T|X, the Centro, or the Treo 700p smartphone.

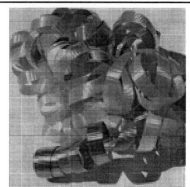

Figure 70. Bitmap: 1X, 16-Bit Color.

Step 20. Save your changes up to this point by pressing **Ctrl+S**, and then close all the bitmaps you've created.

Step 21. Return to **Form 1000**. In the Toolbox, look for the **Form Bitmap** button. Click it, and then click and drag in the upper left corner of the form under the title bar. Note that there's a small shaded box (surrounded by blue dots) that serves as a placeholder on the form.

Also, look in the Properties section. Note that the **Bitmap ID** property reads 0. That means it has not been assigned.

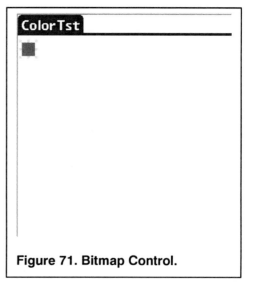

Figure 71. Bitmap Control.

Step 22. Change the **Bitmap ID** property to **1000**, the value for the bitmap we created earlier in this exercise. The placeholder will be replaced with the highest-defined bitmap family. In this case, since we did a 16-bit bitmap, that pops into place. Had we only defined, say, a 16-gray bitmap, that would have popped in, instead.

Step 23. Save your work by pressing **Ctrl+S** on your keyboard.

Step 24. Compile this Palm project and install it on the Garnet OS Simulator, and run it. You should see the bitmap show in bright, beautiful color.

Step 25. The Garnet OS Simulator will also emulate all the other color depths for this application. Right-click on the Simulator and you'll see a pop-up menu; choose **Settings** →

Figure 72. Form With Color Bitmap.

Display → **Color Depth** and from there, you can choose each of the five bitmap families we defined, from 2 colors (black & white) all the way up to 16-bit color.

Step 26. If you have a Palm device, install this application on your Palm device and see what color depth is supported.

What About Double-Density Graphics?

While we had a 160 x 160 bitmap for the ColorTst application, it was just a bit blocky, wasn't it? Better devices such as the Centro and T|X can handle the finer resolution of 320 x 320. Remember that if you're designing graphics for a double-density device, you've got to:

- Produce a version of your bitmaps that are **twice the size** of your "regular" bitmaps.

- Import such bitmaps using the "2X" bitmap families (preferably *2X, 256 Colors* or *2X, 16-Bit RGB*).

135

I will leave it to you as an exercise to try this on your own, defining a bitmap as 280 x 280 instead of 140 x 140 (like in my ribbons image), and then having your ColorTst application present that double-density image instead.

Multiple Bitmap Families Apply To Icons Also

If you plan on having your Palm application run on multiple types of Palm devices, you should consider creating multiple bitmap families for your icons. If you open up the Palm OS Resource Manager and look in the Files section to the right of the screen, you'll notice the first resource is **App Icon Bitmap**. This is the very same bitmap that appears on your Palm desktop when you're ready to tap and start an application.

The App Icon Bitmap resource is subdivided into resource ID 1000 (for the larger icon bitmaps, the ones used almost always) and resource ID 1001 (for the smaller icon bitmaps which are displayed if a user sets their Palm desktop to show application icons in a list mode.

As with any other bitmaps, you can choose to import your own custom bitmap patterns in for the icon resources. But take a look at the icon bitmaps predefined with each new project, so you can see what the bitmap dimensions are (that is, their width by height). If you import too large a bitmap it won't quite fit on the Palm desktop.

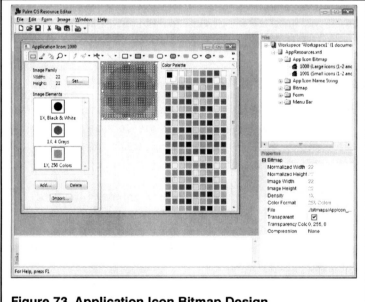

Figure 73. Application Icon Bitmap Design.

11. Detecting Screen Taps

Most Palm controls such as buttons have their own built-in logic for detecting when the screen (or "digitizer", Palm's technical term) has been tapped. But what if you're writing a game and you want to be able to detect when a bitmap or portion of the screen not handled by a Palm control has been tapped? What if all you want is to detect an exact x and y coordinate so you can respond as you wish?

Happily, the Palm OS platform has two ways in which you can detect taps. You can either use what are called gadgets, or you can simply read the event handler's x and y values to determine where a tap occurred. In my own experience, the second approach is a little more reliable. I once wrote a pocket version of the Concentration memory card match game using 25 "gadgets" (look it up in Palm's Help) and – because of a bug in Palm's compiler – the functions to evaluate which gadget had been tapped were not reliable. Besides, when reading the direct x and y coordinates, there's no need to create a pointer variable to the gadget object, nor to have to do any of the associated manipulations.

Simply put, to determine whether a certain portion of the Palm screen has been tapped, you only need to check whether this Boolean condition is true:

$$(xbound_{left} <= x_{tapped} <= xbound_{right})$$

AND

$$(ybound_{lower} <= y_{tapped} <= ybound_{upper})$$

In other words, if the "x" coordinate is between the left and right boundaries of an area and the "y" coordinate is between the lower and upper boundaries of an area, then the user's tap can be used to trigger a function call associated with that area (such as the area of a bitmap of a button) of the Palm screen.

As mentioned above, if you're really curious about what gadgets are, I'll leave it up to you to consult Palm's API documentation (in the Help facility) or consult another text. This chapter will focus exclusively on detecting taps from the event handler.

Exercise P

In this exercise we're going to create a simple tap detection Palm program. Its sole purpose will be to display where, on the screen, you have tapped. You can incorporate the logic from this project into Palm projects of your own, particularly games.

Remember that regardless of whether you're working with single or double density bitmaps, the coordinate system is still 160 x 160 pixels.

Please start GDS and create a new Palm project called "TapRead".

Step 1. In the **C/C++ Projects** window, click on the [+] in front of the **rsc** node until you see **AppResources.xrd**. Double-click on **AppResources.xrd** to open the Palm OS Resource Editor.

Step 2. Under **Files** (right half of screen), be sure **AppResources.xrd** is highlighted, then right-click on that node. On the pop-up menu, choose **New Resource**.

Step 3. On the **New Resource** dialog that shows, choose **Alert** then click **New**. We are going to create a custom alert.

Step 4. Change the **Title** property to say *"You tapped at..."*

Step 5. Change the Message property to read "x= ^ 1, y= ^ 2". Recall that the " ^ 1" and " ^ 2" are placeholders for whatever is passed in. We are going to exclude the " ^ 3" that we used in previous exercises because we don't need it.

Step 6. Press **Ctrl+S** to save your work and then close the Palm OS Resource Editor.

Step 7. Back in the C/C++ Projects Window, double-click on AppMain.c to open it in the main workspace.

Step 8. Locate the Internal Constants section near the top of the file and after the fourth #define, add the following lines of code:

```
#define myAlert 1000

Int16 xtap;        // x coordinate for tap
Int16 ytap;        // y coordinate for tap
Char  xstr[5];     // string representation of tapped x location
Char  ystr[5];     // string representation of tapped y location
```

The first line, of course, is a constant to point to our custom alert.

The next two lines we'll use to hold the the x and y tap coordinates.

The last two lines will hold string representations of xtap and ytap, for the custom alert.

Step 9. Scroll down a ways to the function **MainFormHandleEvent**. After the case leg for **frmOpenEvent**, add the following new case leg for **penDownEvent**:

```
case penDownEvent:
    xtap = pEvent->screenX;
    ytap = pEvent->screenY;
    StrIToA(xstr, xtap);
    StrIToA(ystr, ytap);
    FrmCustomAlert(myAlert, xstr, ystr, "");
    handled = true;
    break;
```

Step 10. Save the project, compile it, and install it to the Garnet OS Simulator. Then start application **TapRead**.

As with the very first project we did, you see the greeting, "Hello, World!" But tap anywhere on the screen in the Simulator and an alert appears showing where you tapped. Tapping the farthest upper left corner will show "x=0, y=0". Tapping the exact middle of screen will show "x=79, y=79", or similar numbers. Tapping the lowest right corner will show "x=159, y=159".

Figure 74. TapRead In Use.

139

Application For Reading Tap Coordinates

So, you may be wondering, how would you use this? Well, consider my example earlier in chapter – a Concentration memory match card game. Suppose your game has 25 boxes in a 5 x 5 grid, and each box in the grid is 30 by 20 pixels:

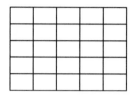

The total width of the game board is 5 x 30 pixels or 150 pixels – which fits snugly into the 160 pixel width. The total height of the game board is 5 x 20 pixels. Since the game board splits the remaining 150 x 150 screen in half, you'll want to check the **screenX** and **screenY** variables for the following:

To detect a **column**:

- **Column #1:** 5 >= screenX >= 35

- **Column #2:** 36 >= screenX >= 65

- **Column #3:** 64 >= screenX >= 95

- **Column #4:** 96 >= screenX >= 125

- **Column #5:** 126 >= screenX >= 155

To detect a **row**:

- **Row #1:** 25 >= screenY >= 45

- **Row #2:** 46 >= screenY >= 65

- **Row #3:** 66 >= screenY >= 85

- **Row #4:** 86 >= screenY >= 105

- **Row #5:** 104 >= screenY >= 125

So if you wanted to determine a particular box number based on a row and column, this is how the calculations would work:

Box #1 = Row 1, Column 1 = (5 x (1 - 1) + 1 = 1

Box #2 = Row 1, Column 2 = (5 x (1 - 1) + 2 = 1

Box #3 = Row 1, Column 3 = (5 x (1 - 1) + 3 = 1

Box #4 = Row 1, Column 4 = (5 x (1 - 1) + 4 = 1

Box #5 = Row 1, Column 5 = (5 x (1 - 1) + 5 = 1

and on Row 2:

Box #6 = Row 2, Column 1 = (5 x (2 - 1) + 1 = 6

Box #7 = Row 2, Column 2 = (5 x (2 - 1) + 2 = 7

and then moving down to Row 3:

Box #11 = Row 3, Column 1 = (5 x (3 - 1) + 1 = 11

And so on, through Box #25.

To review, if you have a bitmap on your screen that represents a control and you want to detect that it's been tapped:

- Be sure you trap a **penDownEvent** in your event handler.

- Capture the values of **pEvent->screenX** and **pEvent->screenY** to global or local variables for testing.

- See if the values of variables you saved off are between the highest and lowest values for the x and y coordinates of your bitmap, **PLUS the height and width of the bitmap.** Got it?

12. Testing & Debugging Tips

I guarantee that before too long, diving into writing Palm software, you'll run into some problems getting your programs to work. And you'll be frustrated with the GDS system because, in some ways, it's actually quite primitive. It is not like using Microsoft's comfy Visual Studio with IntelliSense for everything, and breakpoints you can set on the fly, and stuff like that.

I was hoping that the Eclipse®-based GDS system – and PODS (the Palm OS Development Suite) before that – would be a bit more refined. They are not. In the over four years I've spent messing around writing Palm software, I have had to be not a little bit devious to get my programs tested, or to figure out where a bug is.

This chapter and the next chapter, **Error Messages**, are probably going to be the most important chapters in this book. I can tell you that from doing research on the World Wide Web, I have not seen anything resembling a comprehensive fatal error message database, and that was one of the strongest motivations I had for writing this book. What in the world does "Free handle" mean? Or "Bad window"? Or "Invalid pointer?" How does one go about isolating a problem? How does one fix a problem?

I suppose that this chapter will be the combined years of wisdom I've gained as a software developer in other languages, because when you get right down to it, most programming languages are about the same. And you'll almost certainly have to be creative to get your software working.

This is even more the case because I have observed what I thought were bugs in the Garnet Development Suite – when I've coded something expecting a certain behavior and gotten something quite different. One thing to remember is that unlike in mathematics, there may be several ways you can resolve a bug in Palm C, so don't burn up too much time trying to get your handy-dandy method to work – it may be something you can't fix.

The tips in this chapter aren't going to be presented in any particular order, so be sure to just read 'em all through. I guarantee you'll find something helpful somewhere, somehow.

Define A Custom Alert First

In addition to communicating information to a user of your Palm application, custom alerts have been invaluable for me as a Palm developer. You can use custom alerts to mark the beginning of a function's firing:

```
FrmCustomAlert(myAlert, "Starting Card Shuffle", "", "");
```

You can use it to mark when you expect to be leaving a function:

```
FrmCustomAlert(myAlert, "Leaving Player Init", "", "");
```

You can use it to check the current value of a numeric variable, but you'll need to remember to define a string variable to convert the number to first:

```
Int16  Points;
Char Points_Str[10];

// then elsewhere in the code:
StrIToA(Points_Str, Points);
FrmCustomAlert(myAlert, "Value of Points is:", Points_Str, "");
```

That raises an important point about using custom alerts to display values – you have to convert any non-string value to a string – you cannot, for example, do this:

```
Int8  StartFlag = 0;

// this needs a string variable
FrmCustomAlert(myAlert, "StartFlag=", StartFlag, "");
```

This may involve some gymnastics to accomplish for some values, but it can be done.

Narrow Down Errors By "Whittling"

If you have a function that has a large number of lines and your program dies with a fatal error (that sounds so serious, doesn't it?), tracking it down is best accomplished by narrowing or "whittling" down where the error occurred. Place a custom alert after the first line of the function, then compile and run the program. Assuming you see the custom alert, you can rule out that the first line has caused the problem.

So you move that custom alert to the next line and, again, compile the program and run it in the Garnet OS Emulator. If it doesn't die, then move the custom alert after the third line. Then the fourth. Then the fifth.

Yes, it's not a fun process. Remember that deal at the beginning of the book where I said you have to have patience? Using this debugging method is one of those times.

Function Not Working? Start Over With a Duplicate

Let's say you've been working for days on a function to do something really tricky. You've not been able to get it to work at all, and you're really frustrated.

Make a copy of the function and add "Old" to the name of the function. For example, if you have a function "PickPuzzle" and it's not working, copy all the code to another function called "PickPuzzleOld" and don't touch it. Then start experimenting with the original version of the function. Start removing lines one by one until you figure out why that fatal error occurred.

Take Breaks – Let Your Brain Figure It Out

Our brains don't all work the same way. Some of us need to sleep on a problem. If you find yourself staring at your computer screen, stuck, then stop yourself – take a breather. Close the program, go grab lunch, take a nap, do something that makes you feel good.

I found that returning to a Palm project after letting it go for a day or two allowed me to take a fresh look at it, and in the vast majority of cases, whatever I was stuck on resolved itself.

Back Up Your Work!

This is not exactly a debugging point, but it is important. With CD and DVD burners in just about every PC, you have no excuse for not making a copy of your Palm projects. Why? Because once in a while, hard drives or motherboards go bad, and they will usually "wait" until the very worst time – like when you're about to finish a key part of your project.

Look At Your Old Projects – Reuse Your Code

Save all your old Palm projects – you'll find some routines that you may find easier that rewriting them from scratch. Of course, you may decide that – for performance reasons – it would be better to rewrite that dice rolling routine. That's fine. The point is that once you've gone to the trouble of figuring out a particular problem, you can benefit from it over and over again. Copy your own code!

Look Online For Examples

The great thing about the Palm community is that it's so large. You can find web sites, blogs, and other resources with code segments that may describe how to do the very thing you've been wanting to do.

Go to a search engine and type either a Palm API function name (e.g., TimGetSeconds) or some other piece of your code (like a variable type or something) and then start reading. You may have to look a while before you find something to solve your problem, and your answer may actually involve two or three different pages or pieces of insight. You may have to craft multiple ideas into a new solution. If you're an experienced programmer of any kind, you should be okay looking at other examples.

Don't Bother Using The "Run" Menu

I know, I know – why would Palm include debugging if it doesn't work? Maybe I'm just dense, I don't know. I have never been able to get the Run menu to work.

Watch Those Handles!

Watch your handles! If you have too many handles (that is, you leave extras or re-create them twice because you didn't check for a first time) you'll get fatal chunk errors when you leave your application. The environment (apparently) counts the number of chunks and if it finds too many (memory leaks) it will complain. This is a really easy error to make, particularly if you're a beginner.

Test On Actual Palm Devices, When Possible

While the Garnet OS Simulator is a great tool for checking your work in the short term, it is very much to your advantage – especially if you plan on marketing your Palm application – to test your creation on actual Palm devices. You can create your own "test bed" by getting on eBay and acquiring several second-hand, older devices. Test your application on every one. Or, if you don't feel like doing that, find several friends or business associates of yours that have Palm devices and HotSync your creation to them for them to test.

13. Fatal Error Message Lookup

As far as I'm concerned, this chapter alone is worth the price of this book. In every other Palm book I've reviewed – and I've seen quite a few – no one has a tabulated list of fatal error messages that kill a Palm program. A fatal error, in case you haven't had the pleasure, is an unanticipated condition that causes your Palm device to lock up and reset itself – the equivalent of the ol' Windows "blue-screen of death".

But that's not all there is to this chapter – alongside many of the error messages I also present suggestions on how to resolve the error, things you can try. This is a list that I dearly wished I'd had when I was writing my first Palm projects; I had to guess how to correct the problems with trial and error. You may still have to use trial and error on your own problems, but at least this chapter will give you a headstart. I would like to point out that all the errors in this chapter, I have received *personally*.

Messages are listed in alphabetical order, and when they show up running the Garnet OS Emulator, show in a dialog that looks like this:

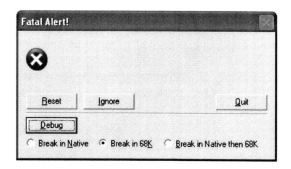

Expect to see this a lot when you're starting out.

Also, please realize that this is *not an exhaustive list* of all the errors you may encounter when debugging your Palm program. These just happened to be the ones I ran into when learning how to write Palm software for myself.

Most fatal errors fall into one of the following classes:

- **Pointer values that are null or unexpected, either because you forgot to set a value using one of Palm's API functions to find them, or because something else went wrong in your logic.**

- **Incorrect or incomplete memory handle operations – such as leaving a handle locked when it should be unlocked, or not locking a memory chunk.**

- **Record handling errors – such as forgetting to unlock a record before leaving a program.**

- **Referring to a resource or control by the wrong number (the 4-digit resource ID).**

With experience you'll begin to realize what you've done and where to look for mistakes.

Bad window

Why this error probably happened: You performed an operation associated with a form – such as drawing a bitmap or referring to a text field – before the form was actually opened with a **FrmOpenForm** function call. In other words, you're trying to work with a form that isn't there. This is a mistake you could make if you're trying to initialize a form for its first display to your end user. Don't get ahead of yourself. Look at where the **FrmDrawForm** function is called – that's where you should (timing-wise) place any calls to routines to work with controls on the form.
How you could possibly fix it: Move any operations associated with controls on the form to a point later than the call to **FrmDrawForm**. This includes calls to **WinDrawBitmap** or similar functions.

Chunk over-locked

Why this error probably happened: Think about the Palm's memory management scheme. In some cases, you have to lock a chunk of memory, such as for changing a text string on an editable field, before you can manipulate it. In this particular case, you probably have two calls to **MemHandleLock** (which locks a memory chunk), which isn't necessary. This message is the same as saying, "It's already locked, dum-dum."

How you could possibly fix it: Look for an extra call to **MemHandleLock** and remove it.
See also: "Chunk under-locked."

Chunk under-locked

Why this error probably happened: You probably have a call to **MemHandleUnlock** (which unlocks a memory chunk), which – for some reason isn't necessary. The first time I saw this message, I had the following series of function calls: **DmGetRecord, MemHandleLock, DmWrite, MemPtrUnlock, DmReleaseRecord,** and **MemHandleUnlock**.
How you could possibly fix it: Look for an extra call to **MemHandleUnlock** and remove it.
See also: "Chunk over-locked."

Computed rectangle too far left

Why this error probably happened: You're trying to move a character string into a text field that's too small. (Helpful message text, isn't it?)
How you could possibly fix it: Make the text field larger (click on a blue-dot boundary for the text field and pull it so it's larger).

Err getting rec

Why this error probably happened: Short for "error getting record". I saw this error when I tried a write operation to a record I'd locked (using the **DmGetRecord** and then **DmWrite** functions).
How you could possibly fix it: Make sure your Palm database (PDB file) was correctly found and opened by your program, then make sure you've requested the correct record number (that is, if you know there's only 2 records in the database, don't ask for a record number 18 since it doesn't exist).

Field cannot be editable

Why this error probably happened: You're working with a text field that has an Editable property value of true, and you're using the function **FldSetTextPtr**, which is supposed to be used only with text fields that have an Editable property of false – that is uneditable or for display only.
How you could possibly fix it: Two options: (a) change the Editable property of the target field to false, or (b) if you want the user to be able to change the field (such as if you're setting a series of default values for first use of your program),

use the **FldSetTextHandle** function. But this second approach is a little more involved, because you need to: create a new memory handle, lock it, set the resulting pointer to a character string, work with the string, and then unlock the handle.

See also: "Field is using a handle – setting the pointer is invalid."

Field is using a handle – setting the pointer is invalid

Why this error probably happened: This error is the functional opposite of the "Field cannot be editable" error above – only in this case, you're probably working with a text field that has an Editable property value of true and you're treating it as if it were false by using the function **FldSetTextPtr**, which is only for text fields that aren't editable. In other words, the text field is associated with a memory handle that's currently in use.

How you could possibly fix it: Two options: (a) change the Editable property of the target field to false, or (b) if you're only using the text field for display only, use the **FldSetTextPtr** function instead.

See also: "Field cannot be editable."

Field object improperly locked

Why this error probably happened: Likely the result of locking a field incorrectly. The code sequence that gave me this originally was:

```
// init the entry field
fld = FrmGetObjectPtr(pForm, FrmGetObjectIndex(pForm,fldAdd1));

// 1. get the handle (w/o lock)
fldH = FldGetTextHandle(fld);
FldSetTextHandle(fld, NULL);

// 2. make changes here
textH = MemHandleNew(StrLen("000") + 1);
text = MemHandleLock(textH);

// 3. move the new text to the field
FldSetText(fld, textH, 0, 4);

// 4. draw it now
FldDrawField(fld);
```

Note what I did: I got a locked handle to a text field and cleared it out (set it to NULL). Then I created a new memory handle 4 bytes long and tried to move it to the field pointer ("fld").

How you could possibly fix it: Go back and look at the use of your calls to FldGetTextHandle, FldSetTextHandle, MemHandleNew, MemHandleLock, and

FldSetText. One of your uses of these functions is the culprit. You'll probably have to use the process of elimination to figure out what the problem is.

Form already loaded

Why this error probably happened: You called the function **FrmInitForm** more than once for the same form. When you "init" a form, you're loading it to Palm's memory and it stays there until it's unloaded explicitly or the program ends.
How you could possibly fix it: Look through your code and remove any extra calls to **FrmInitForm**.

Free handle

Why this error probably happened: This is Palm's way of saying you've freed a handle that's already free. In other words, you likely have two function calls to **MemHandleFree**, one or more of which you don't need.
How you could possibly fix it: Look for anyplace you call **MemHandleFree** and delete any extra instances.

Invalid insertion point position

Why this error probably happened: Likely happened when you were running a form with a text field. It was the first time the form appeared and you tapped the field. This, oddly, may have happened because the Font property for the text field is for a font that doesn't fit the size of the field. For example, the LED font used by the Palm calculator application is twice as large as that of the Standard font – it won't fit.
How you could possibly fix it: Change the font to Standard or a smaller font.

Invalid read from HHHHHHHH (8-digit hex number)

Why this error probably happened: This error occurred when you were likely trying to read a record from a Palm database file (.PDB) in your program. When I got this error originally, it was because I was trying to read a database line into a record that had character strings of indeterminate length (**Char* somename**) rather that a fixed length (**Char somename[40]**).
How you could possibly fix it: Look at the typedef you have defined for your record structure, and make sure every character string is defined as fixed-length with Char and brackets around the length.

`Invalid ptr: ` *`xxxxxxxx`* `(8 hex digits)`

Why this error probably happened: This is a very common error for C beginners. It may mean that (a) you're trying to work with a pointer variable that's null, (b) that you're trying to work with a variable that's a part of a record and you either coded "->" when you mean a "." or the other way around, or (c) you're working with a string variable coded with **Char somename[20];** when it should be the indeterminate length string **Char* somename;**. There may also be other reasons, but suffice it to say you're doing something naughty with a pointer variable.

How you could possibly fix it: Several ways: (a) make sure the pointer variable has an actual value by checking it with an **if** block, (b) switch "->" to "." and see if that helps, or switch "." to "->" and see if that helps, (c) change the definition of your character variable from a fixed-length (**Char somename[30]**) to an indeterminate length (**Char* somename**).

`Invalid size`

Why this error probably happened: This is likely the result of trying to stuff a character string into a text field that's too small to handle it.

How you could possibly fix it: If you've called the function **FldSetText** in your program, look carefully at the third and fourth arguments – chances are you have one or both values don't belong there.

`Minor error while exiting app: un-freed chunk at 0x`*`HHHHHHHH`*`, size ` *`NN`*
`(ownerID Q)`

Why this error probably happened: This is one of the ugliest messages the Palm folks could have created, and it's not helpful. The "*HHHHHHHH*" is a series of 8 hex digits representing a memory address, the "*NN*" refers to the size of the memory chunk in question, and "*Q*" is the owner ID (which you usually don't have to worry about). The net of this message is this: by the time the application ended, you had forgotten to free a memory chunk using the **MemHandleFree** function.

How you could possibly fix it: Look through your code for where you use **MemHandleLock** and be sure to place a **MemHandleFree** call closer to it. All handles must be freed before you leave a Palm application. (And, as far as I can tell, there is no significance to Palm's use of the word "minor" in this error message. An error is an error.)

```
No visible lines to allocate
```

Why this error probably happened: The text field's Visible Lines property is set to 0.

How you could possibly fix it: Change the value of Visible Lines to 1 or a larger number. Also, check that Usable is checked, Editable is checked, and Single Line is checked, and that Max Lines To Show is set to 1.

```
Null form
```

Why this error probably happened: You have a form pointer variable that's null or uninitialized. You probably forgot to set it before attempting an operation with the form (such as redrawing it).

How you could possibly fix it: Simple – at the top of your function, set your form pointer variable to the result of the **FrmGetActiveForm** function. All actions performed after that should work fine.

```
Object #AAAA in form #FFFF is missing
```

Why this error probably happened: You have an instruction that refers to a control ID on the form with number *FFFF* (4-digit number) that, to Palm, doesn't exist. What you probably did was to define a constant with a particular resource ID number (*AAAA*), and then you changed something later and forgot to go back and change the constant. Or if you're not using a constant, you're simply using the wrong number.

How you could possibly fix it: If you're using a constant, go back and make sure it matches the number for the control in the Palm OS Resource Editor. If you're not using a constant, check the number for the resource you're using, because you probably changed it at some point.

```
Odd aligned read from xxxxxxxx (series of 8 hex digits)
```

Why this error probably happened: Palm's memory management scheme is rather picky. When I first observed this error, it was when I was trying to code a timer loop for a game. Another thing to consider is that you might have passed a UInt32 variable to a function that was expecting a smaller number as an argument – such as **StrIToA**, which I used. A UInt32 variable is a 32-bit – or 4-byte number. Under the covers, sometimes Palm tries to do things along 4-byte boundaries, or every 4th byte. (Don't ask me to explain it, I couldn't help you.)

How you could possibly fix it: Try using a different numeric variable such as an Int32 (a signed integer), or Int16 (a smaller signed integer).

```
Ptr is handle
```

Why this error probably happened: You tried to use a Palm function on a variable defined as a pointer when it's actually a handle. I originally got this error when I had defined a variable "recordH" as a **MemHandle** (memory handle variable) and then tried to use the **MemPtrUnlock** function with it (which expects pointers, not handles).

How you could possibly fix it: Look at your variable definitions and see what you meant to do. If you meant to define a pointer, do so, and then use a pointer-related function. If you meant to define a memory handle, do so and then use a memory handle-related function. The two types of variables are similar but are NOT interchangeable: a pointer refers to a location in memory (in hexadecimal). A handle is a randomly assigned internal ID number (also in hexadecimal) but it has no bearing on memory size.

```
Records left busy in closed unprotected DB
```

Why this error probably happened: You probably (a) opened a Palm database (a .PDB file), (b) locked a record using **DmGetRecord**, and (c) closed the database with **DmCloseDatabase** without unlocking the record you were using.

How you could possibly fix it: If all you need to do is look at a record (in read-only mode), consider using the function **DmQueryRecord** instead. Otherwise, look at your code and add a call to **DmReleaseRecord** for the record in the database you were using.

See also: "Records left locked in closed unprotected DB."

```
Records left locked in closed unprotected DB
```

Why this error probably happened: You probably (a) opened a Palm database (a .PDB file), (b) locked a record using **DmGetRecord**, and (c) closed the database with **DmCloseDatabase** without unlocking the record you were using.

How you could possibly fix it: If all you need to do is look at a record (in read-only mode), consider using the function **DmQueryRecord** instead. Otherwise, look at your code and add a call to **DmReleaseRecord** for the record in the database you were using.

See also: "Records left busy in closed unprotected DB."

```
Resource for app form NNNN not found
```

Why this error probably happened: You either changed the resource ID (a 4-digit number *NNNN*) for one of your forms or you've defined a constant that refers to a 4-digit number for a form that doesn't exist.

How you could possibly fix it: Look at the number for the resource ID for the form where the program blows up. Then open your Palm OS Resource Editor and look for the form you thought you were accessing. You either need to change the resource ID for the form in the editor, or change your code.

```
Text block size smaller than text
```

Why this error probably happened: You're trying to put a text string into a locked memory handle that's not large enough.
How you could possibly fix it: Look at your use of the MemHandleNew function – if the number you're passing in is too small, make it larger.

14. Working With Palm Databases

Some applications you may write may require a capability for saving information once the application has been closed. If, for example, you write a game that has puzzles or questions stored, you'll need a way of saving those and retrieving them later. Or if you're writing an application that stores information, you'll need a way of storing that information as database records.

Palm's architecture is such that there is a way of holding such information, and that is as a PDB file, or Palm DataBase (hence the three-letter abbreviation). A PDB may sound sophisticated, but in actuality, it's just a very specially formatted binary file. You don't even really need to understand the format of the file unless your Palm application is going to have information already stored – if your program starts with an empty database, you can create that database on the fly.

In this chapter, I'm going to cover the basics of working with Palm databases.

Database Pointers

The first thing to know about Palm databases is that they have their own special pointers, similar in function but differently defined than those for C. A Palm database pointer is called the inelegantly named "DmOpenRef". Declarations for Palm databases would look like these:

```
DmOpenRef mydb;
DmOpenRef puzzlesdb;
DmOpenRef hiscores;
```

Note that unlike C variables, these database pointer variables *do not* require an asterisk (*) preceding the name.

Record Structures

Typically, a database is associated with a set of records of fixed length – that is, all records in the database will be 40 bytes, 120 bytes, 15 bytes, or whatever you need. In many cases, a single record will be subdivided into fields. If, for example, you wanted to have a high score database for a game program, you might define a record structure like this:

```
struct HiScoreRec {
    Char player_init[31];
    Char score[11];
    Char date[11];
};
```

Once a structure is defined, you will need a pointer variable for that structure, because that will be how Palm "talks" to the database. Continuing the illustration, for the structure above, one such pointer variable might be:

```
struct HiScoreRec *myHSrecPtr;
struct HiScoreRec  myHSrec;        // this is for sizeof calls
```

Note that we define an "ordinary" record variable; this will solely be for when calls to sizeof are needed; you'll observe this later.

We're now ready to actually open a database.

Creating A Database On The Fly

For some applications, you may want to start with an empty database. You can create a new database on the fly. But before you do, you should check for the presence of the database first. This logic plays out as follows:

```
// Try opening the database
// If it's there, perform any initialization processing and continue
// If it's not there, define it (and seed it with anything you need)
```

On the next page is a routine that demonstrates this logic more fully.

```
void LoadOptions() {

    DmOpenRef myOptionsDB;
    MemHandle myHandle;
    Err myErr;
    Err errflag = 0;
    Int16 ptr = 0;

    myOptionsDB = DmOpenDatabaseByTypeCreator('DATA', 'ABCD', dmModeReadWrite);

    if (myOptionsDB) {

        // Read the current options
        myHandle = DmQueryRecord(myOptionsDB, ptr);
        myHSrecPtr = MemHandleLock(myHandle);
        // (manipulate any record structure variables here)
        MemHandleUnlock(myHandle);

    } else {

        //*************************************
        // Doesn't exist, create it
        //*************************************

        errflag = DmCreateDatabase(0, "Game Options", 'ABCD', 'DATA', false);

        if (errflag != errNone) {

            FrmCustomAlert(myAlert, "Unexpected error", "", "");

        } else {

            // Now, open the database for use
            myOptionsDB = DmOpenDatabaseByTypeCreator('DATA', 'ABCD', dmModeReadWrite);

            // Write a basic record - using DmStrCopy instead of DmWrite.
            myHandle = DmNewRecord(myOptionsDB, &ptr, sizeof(myHSrec));
            myHSrecPtr = MemHandleLock(myHandle);
            DmStrCopy(myHSrecPtr, 31, "000");
            MemHandleUnlock(myHandle);
            DmReleaseRecord(myOptionsDB, ptr, true);

        }

    }


    //****************************************************
    // Through with it, close it until next time
    //****************************************************
    myErr = DmCloseDatabase(myOptionsDB);
    if (myErr) {
        FrmCustomAlert(myAlert, "Error closing Options Database.", "", "");
    }

}
```

Let's take a closer look at this routine. First, after the variable declarations, there is this instruction:

```
myOptionsDB = DmOpenDatabaseByTypeCreator('DATA', 'ABCD', dmModeReadWrite);
```

The **DmOpenDatabaseByTypeCreator** function attempts to open a database. The three arguments for this function are the **resource type** (almost always set to 'DATA' for these purposes), the **creator ID** (a unique 4-character identifier that prevents Palm programs and databases from stepping on each other), and the **access mode** (read/write or read only). The result is passed to a local DmOpenRef variable in this example, but in real-life programming, you would probably want to have your database variable as a global variable (defined at the top of the C source code ahead of all the functions) so if more than one routine needs to get at it, they can all do so.

This is followed by an if-check to see if anything was returned. If the DmOpenDatabaseByTypeCreator function found a database with the creator ID "ABCD" (in this example), it would return that to the variable myOptionsDB. If it didn't find anything, a null value would be returned.

If a non-null value was returned – that is, if the database was found on the Palm device – then in the following lines:

```
// Read the current options
myHandle = DmQueryRecord(myOptionsDB, ptr);
myOptionsDB = MemHandleLock(myHandle);
// (manipulate any record structure variables here)
MemHandleUnlock(myHandle);
```

you can read the contents of the record associated with the database. The first line uses the function **DmQueryRecord** to look at the record number referenced by the variable ptr (in this case). So if ptr is equal to 0, it would get the *first* record in the database (remember that record numbers like everything else in C are zero-based). DmQueryRecord does not lock a record; it just does a quick "in-and-out" read and sends the result to a memory handle variable, in this case, myHandle.

In the second line, the handle is locked and the resulting pointer is directed to the database pointer variable myOptionsDB.

Between the second line and the third line, you would read the content of any variables in the record structure. Using our high-score record structure, we could grab the first high-score record into locally defined variables as follows:

160

```
StrCopy(playerName, myHSrecPtr->player);
StrCopy(hiScore, myHSrecPtr->score);
StrCopy(scoreDate, myHSrecPtr->date);
```

If the result of **DmOpenDatabaseByTypeCreator** is a null, then we'll have to create a new database. That's accomplished with this line:

```
errflag = DmCreateDatabase(0, "Game Options", 'ABCD', 'DATA', false);
```

The **DmCreateDatabase** function does exactly what the name suggests – it creates a new Palm database using these five arguments:

- The **device** on which you want to create the database – almost always 0, representing the Palm device itself (rather than an external card)

- A **name** that will appear in the Palm's "Info" list of program information. This may be up to 31 characters long.

- A unique **creator ID** – a 4-character identifier to keep programs and databases from stepping on each other

- A **resource type**, usually "DATA"

- A fifth parameter, almost always set to false, to indicate this is **NOT a resource database** being created.

Note that with the next lines:

```
if (errflag != errNone) {

    FrmCustomAlert(myAlert, "Unexpected error", "", "");
```

we check to see if our database creation succeeded or failed. This is wise to check for, even if it's unlikely to happen.

If there is no error on the creation of the database, then the database needs to be opened for use – the creation operation alone doesn't open it. That explains the second **DmOpenDatabaseByTypeCreator** instruction.

Following the opening of the new database, in this particular routine, I have processing writing a "seed" first record with this instruction:

```
DmStrCopy(myHSrecPtr, 31, "000");
```

The **DmStrCopy** function is similar to the StrCopy function except that DmStrCopy copies a string to a specific place – that is, a specific *position number* – in a database record. In the example above, the three arguments are the **record pointer** (myHSrecPtr), the **offset** to the place to write (31 characters, or just past the player name character string), and the **string value to write** (in this case, three zeros).

NOTE: If you're a relative beginner to working with Palm databases, I would recommend **storing all data in character strings**, even if the values are numeric. You can take numeric values and run them through Palm functions to convert them to character strings and vice versa. If you're a real genius you can try storing native integer and decimal values bit by bit, but I have a feeling most of you won't really need to do this.

Next follow two important instructions:

```
MemHandleUnlock(myHandle);
DmReleaseRecord(myOptionsDB, ptr, true);
```

The first function, **MemHandleUnlock**, unlocks the memory handle myHandle – that's just part of Palm's picky scheme for memory management – and the second, **DmReleaseRecord**, releases the record.

DmReleaseRecord's three arguments are the database pointer, a variable representing which record number to release (zero-based), and whether the record being released is "dirty" or not – meaning it should be backed up the next time a HotSync is performed.

Once you're through with the database, you must close it using the **DmCloseDatabase** function. This accepts the database pointer variable as its only argument and returns an error pointer (the **Err** type, unique to Palm C). If the Err pointer has a non-null value, an error message is written. Otherwise processing proceeds as normal. (Values for Err indicating various error conditions can be found in Palm's Help documentation.)

Try To Minimize Lines Between Opening and Closing A Database

One coding technique I recommend – try to minimize the number of lines between your opening and closing a database. This is because if your user (for example) closes your application to clear an alert from the Scheduler that came up, you don't want a Fatal Alert to reboot the device.

Also, open the database only when it's really needed. You might create a simple routine – perhaps call it "OpenDatabase" – and call it when you need data from the Palm database. And, likewise, create another routine – called, for example, "CloseDatabase", to close it when you're through.

Creating A Database Containing Records

All very good and nice, but suppose you want to provide a database that *already* contains records? You want to write a quiz or word game that contains clues, for example. That's a bit more challenging, and it requires you to create a Palm database that follows Palm's internal format for databases. Exploring the structure of the Palm database is well beyond the scope of this book; I advise you to search online for information about Palm databases, or even Palm's own API documentation, if you're really curious.

Your best bet for creating a Palm database is with a desktop application that will automatically create the files for you. I have written such an application for the Windows platform using Microsoft Visual Studio 2008, using the Visual Basic language, and I call it **PDBMaker**. On the following pages I include the source code for you to create the program. If you're used to using C++ or another language, the source code should be simple enough that you can figure out the algorithm and adapt it to the language you wish to use.

PDBMaker

Below is the source code for PDBMaker using Microsoft Visual Studio 2008 (.NET). If you do not have Microsoft Visual Studio 2008, you can download the Express version free at **www.microsoft.com/express/vb**. Type carefully!

Step 1. Create a form as shown above. It should have entry fields for an input data file, an output data file, a database name, a creator ID, a record length, and a number of output records. Name each of the controls as labeled below in bold type (with the "txt" and "btn" names).

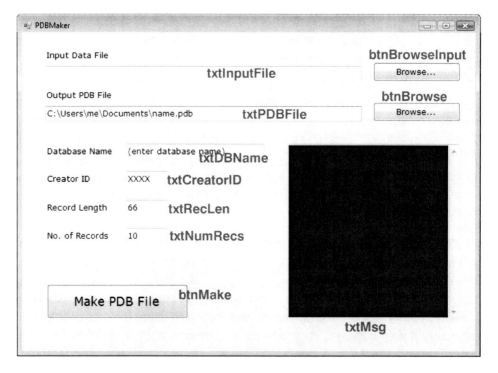

Step 2. Add two controls from the **Dialogs** toolbox. Add a **SaveFileDialog** control and call it **fdSave**. Add an **OpenFileDialog** control and call it **fdOpen**.

Step 3. Double click on the upper **"Browse..."** button (btnBrowseInput) and add the following code:

```
fdOpen.ShowDialog()
If fdOpen.FileName <> "" Then
    txtInputFile.Text = fdOpen.FileName
End If
```

Step 4. Double-click on the lower **"Browse…"** button (btnBrowse) and add the following code:

```
fdSave.ShowDialog()
If fdSave.FileName <> "" Then
    txtPDBFile.Text = fdSave.FileName
End If
```

Step 5. This is the last part of this, but also the longest. Double click on the **"Make PDB File"** button (btnMake) and type *all the code* below.

```
Dim n As Integer
Dim b As Integer                    ' for managing MyBytes(4)

Dim LowByte As String
Dim HexOffset As String
Dim NumRecsHex As String

Dim SerialNumHex As String = ""

Dim TestStr As String = ""

Dim Char4(4) As Char                ' fixed-length strings
Dim Hdr78(78) As Char
Dim Spacer(1) As Char

Dim FullRec(CInt(txtRecLen.Text)) As Char

Dim DataLine As String = ""         ' input
Dim Warned As Boolean = False


' OPEN FILE

Dim ofile As New IO.BinaryWriter(File.OpenWrite(txtPDBFile.Text))
Dim dfile As New IO.StreamReader(txtInputFile.Text)

' WRITE HEADER

DBName = PadRight(txtDBName.Text, 31) & Chr(0)
Attr = Chr(0) & Chr(0)
Ver = Chr(0) & Chr(0)

CrtDate = Chr(0) & Chr(0) & Chr(0) & Chr(0)
ModDate = Chr(0) & Chr(0) & Chr(0) & Chr(0)
BkpDate = Chr(0) & Chr(0) & Chr(0) & Chr(0)

ModNum = Chr(0) & Chr(0) & Chr(0) & Chr(0)
AppInfo = Chr(0) & Chr(0) & Chr(0) & Chr(0)
SortInfo = Chr(0) & Chr(0) & Chr(0) & Chr(0)

DBType = "DATA"
CreatorID = txtCreatorID.Text
UniqueID = Chr(0) & Chr(0) & Chr(0) & Chr(0)
```

```
        OutStr = DBName & Attr & Ver & _
            CrtDate & ModDate & BkpDate & _
            ModNum & AppInfo & SortInfo & _
            DBType & CreatorID & UniqueID

        HdrLen = OutStr.Length

        Hdr78 = OutStr

        ofile.Write(Hdr78)

        txtMsg.Text = txtMsg.Text & "Header written" & vbCrLf


        ' NEXT RECORD LIST ID - USUALLY 0'S

        NextRecID = Chr(0) & Chr(0) & Chr(0) & Chr(0)
        Char4 = NextRecID
        ofile.Write(Char4)

        'UniqueID = Chr(0) & Chr(0) & Chr(0) & Chr(0)


        ' WRITE NUMBER OF RECORDS

        NumRecsHex = Hex(txtNumRecs.Text)
        NumRecsHex = LeftPadZero(NumRecsHex, 4)        ' 4 means four characters like '0000'
        TestStr = RealHex(NumRecsHex)
        Char4 = TestStr
        ofile.Write(Char4)

        'Spacer(0) = Chr(0)
        'Spacer(1) = Chr(0)
        'ofile.Write(Spacer)


        ' WRITE RECORD LIST WITH OFFSETS

        If CInt(txtNumRecs.Text) = 0 Then              ' if empty PDB, use this; this
            FirstEntry = Chr(0) & Chr(0)               ' preserves 4-byte boundaries.
            ofile.Write(FirstEntry)
            ofile.Close()
            MessageBox.Show("Empty PDB file created.")
            Exit Sub
        End If


        AllOffsetsLen = 8 * CInt(txtNumRecs.Text)

        For n = 1 To CInt(txtNumRecs.Text)

            RecOffset(n) = HdrLen + AllOffsetsLen + ((n - 1) * CInt(txtRecLen.Text))
            RecOffset(n) = RecOffset(n) + 6            ' why?
            txtMsg.Text = txtMsg.Text & "Record List Offset At: " & RecOffset(n).ToString
& vbCrLf

        Next
```

166

```
For n = 1 To CInt(txtNumRecs.Text)

    TestStr = Hex(RecOffset(n))

    HexOffset = LeftPadZero(Hex(RecOffset(n)), 8)          ' 00 00 00 00
    txtMsg.Text = txtMsg.Text & "Hex Value: " & HexOffset & vbCrLf       ' chunk ID

    RealHexBytes(HexOffset)              ' Result sent to MyBytes(4)

    For b = 0 To 3
        ofile.Write(CByte(MyBytes(b)))
    Next

    ' Take the serial number for each record, convert it to hex,
    ' pad it to four digits (e.g., '0001') and write it.

    SerialNumHex = RealHex(LeftPadZero(Hex(n), 4))

    ' This next instruction always assumes attribs are 0's and that
    ' there won't be more than 4-bytes' worth of records (typical)
    ' that is, x'FFFF'.

    LowByte = Chr(0) & Chr(0) & SerialNumHex
    Char4 = LowByte

    ofile.Write(Char4)                       'WRITE LOW 4 BYTES

Next


' WRITE DATA RECORDS - If not enough data, write blanks with a caution message

For n = 1 To CInt(txtNumRecs.Text)

    If dfile.Peek > 0 Then
        DataLine = dfile.ReadLine.Trim       ' strip blanks (may change later)
    Else
        If Not Warned Then
            MessageBox.Show("You have fewer lines in your data file than the
number you specified.  Extra lines will be blank records.", "Short Data File",
MessageBoxButtons.OK, MessageBoxIcon.Exclamation)
            DataLine = Space(FullRec.Length)
            Warned = True
        End If
    End If

    If DataLine.Length < CInt(txtRecLen.Text) Then
        OutputRec(n) = DataLine & Nulls(CInt(txtRecLen.Text) - DataLine.Length)
    ElseIf DataLine.Length > CInt(txtRecLen.Text) Then
        OutputRec(n) = DataLine.Substring(0, CInt(txtRecLen.Text))
    Else
        OutputRec(n) = DataLine
    End If

    FullRec = OutputRec(n)               ' padding to full length of record done here.

    ofile.Write(FullRec)

Next
```

167

```
' CLOSE FILES

dfile.Close()
ofile.Close()
MessageBox.Show("PDB file created.")
```

Step 6. While still in the code view, scroll all the way to the top of the code, to where you see the line **Public Class Form1**. Insert a line before that line and type **Imports System.IO**.

Step 7. After the line **Public Class Form1**, type all the following lines. They are very important, so don't miss any!

```
Public RecOffset(100) As Integer
Public OutputRec(100) As String

Public MyBytes(4) As Int16
Public MyChar As Char

Public HdrLen As Integer

Public DBName As String
Public Attr As String
Public Ver As String
Public CrtDate As String
Public ModDate As String
Public BkpDate As String
Public ModNum As String
Public AppInfo As String
Public SortInfo As String
Public DBType As String
Public CreatorID As String
Public UniqueID As String
Public NextRecID As String

Public NumRecs As Integer

Public FirstEntry As String            ' only used if empty

Public OffsetCtr As Integer
Public AllOffsetsLen As Integer

Public OutStr As String
```

Step 8. To compile all this and run it, press the **F5** button on your keyboard or on the menu bar, choose **Debug → Start Debugging**. This will compile the the program and start running it.

Using PDBMaker

PDBMaker is a very primitive application for creating Palm databases or PDB files. Essentially all you do is to choose an input and output file locations, specify the information about the database file, and click a button to create the file.

Step 1. Click the upper **Browse** button on the same line as **Input Data File**. This should point to a Text format file (*.txt) but as long as the contents of the file are ASCII-based text, you may point to a file with any extension you like.

Step 2. Click the lower **Browse** button on the same line as **Output PDB File**. Specify a file name; the extension must be **.pdb**.

Step 3. In the **Database Name** field, type a name for your database. This is not the name of the database file; this is the text that appears when you choose the Info option from your Palm's application menu (from where you usually start programs) to list program information. This may be up to 31 characters long. Choose a descriptive name.

Step 4. In the **Creator ID** field, choose a 4-character creator ID that matches the creator ID you specified in your Palm program (in functions like **DmOpenDatabaseByCreatorID**).

Step 5. In the **Record Length** field, enter the length of each of your records. Be sure the length you enter includes nulls. To find this length, add up all the variable lengths in the record structure to be used to retrieve from and write to this database.

Step 6. In the **No. of Records** field, enter the number of records to be contained in your Palm database.

Step 7. Once you've entered all this information, click the **Make PDB File** button. The black box will fill with green text indicating the offset data for each record in the output file (offsets are beyond the scope of this book).

You can then use the PDB file you've created – while testing with the Palm Emulator, or on your actual Palm device before you're ready to distribute it.

Input For PDBMaker

So what should you use for input to PDBMaker? Your Text file (extension .txt) should contain information that's formatted in *fixed-length columns*. **Do not use the Tab character to create this file or line up the columns; the program won't correctly interpret the Tab characters.** Use the space bar to position columns of text.

Let's suppose we're writing a quiz program that tests users on the 2-letter abbreviations for each of the 50 United States. The record structure for this might look like the following:

```
struct QuizRec {
    Char statename[21];
    Char abbrev[3];
};
```

Remember, if the state can be 20 characters and the abbreviation can be 2 characters, we MUST have one extra space at the end of each variable for the terminating null, per C language rules. So the **statename** variable winds up 21 characters long, and the **abbrev** variable is 3 characters long.

To prepare a text file in Notepad to feed into PDBMaker, you want it to look like Figure 75.

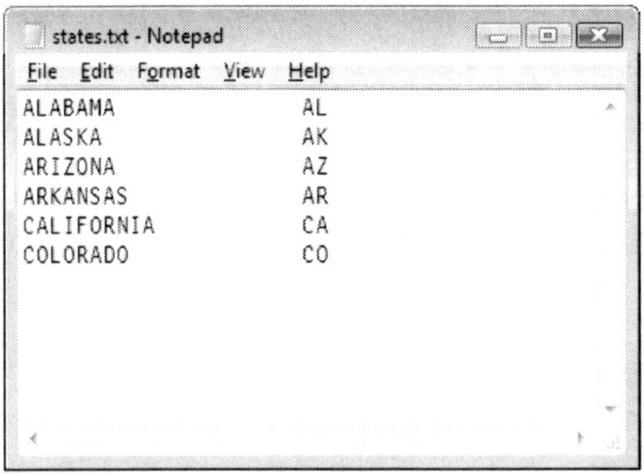

Figure 75. Input File For PDBMaker.

Note that although the names of each state are shorter than 21 characters, each state name is padded with spaces to the right. When your Palm program looks for the state abbreviation, it's going to expect to find 21 characters after the start of each record. You will have to ensure that such spaces are present. I would suggest writing a program, on your own, to automatically generate text files like this. (Exporting directly from Excel will not cut it.)

15. MathLib And FP Numbers

Palm's API has facilities for floating-point number support, but I'll warn you – they're a bit unwieldy and are not especially convenient to use. But you'll need to be comfortable enough knowing how to use them if you plan on writing applications involving floating-point arithmetic.

This is even more important if you want to use the publicly available **MathLib** package. MathLib is a collection of scientific mathematical functions – stuff like sine, cosine, and logarithms – that are not a part of the base Palm API.

One important thing to remember about using MathLib is that it has its own Palm database file (.PRC) that must be distributed with your own application PRC file. If you want to perform floating-point operations but not use the MathLib functions to do it – that is, by using C's own arithmetic function – you do not have to distribute MathLib's PRC file.

Downloading MathLib

You can type "palm mathlib" into any search engine to locate a host of download pages, but I would recommend going to this one in particular:

```
http://www.radiks.net/~rhuebner/mathlib.html
```

In addition to providing the downloadable PRC file, the page itself gives some explanation as to what MathLib is.

MathLib is a stable software package; it has (apparently) not been updated since 2005.

Once you have downloaded the **MathLibSrc.zip** file, extract all the contents and review them. (The MathLib.zip is mainly the executable and doesn't let you see all the functions you can call, so I would recommend downloading MathLibSrc.zip instead. And MathLib.gcc.zip contains even more that you really won't need, so don't bother to download that file either.)

The MathLib package's two most important files are:

- **MathLDoc.htm** – Documentation on the use of MathLib. Very important file – please be sure to read the section "Using MathLib".

- **MathLib.prc** – The Palm PRC database (executable file).

Also included is the **Copying.txt** file, an important file, as it presents the MathLib license agreement (which is actually quite generous).

In addition, unzipping the package file creates an **Rsc** folder (which you won't need) and an **Src** folder (which you will need).

Open the **Src** folder and open the **MathLib.c** file; this file shows you the prototypes for each of the MathLib function. Note that each function accepts a **double** variable and returns a **double** value. You should use the "**.d**" part of the FlpCompDouble union to access double values. See "Declaring Floating Point Variables" in the next section for more information.

Declaring Floating Point Variables

Floating-point (FP) numbers are declared with the data type **FlpCompDouble**. But beware – FlpCompDouble is actually a union. This means that different data share the same physical storage in memory. Here is the definition of FlpCompDouble from the Palm API documentation:

```
typedef union {
  double d;
  FlpDouble fd;
  UInt32 ul[2];
  FlpDoubleBits fdb;
} FlpCompDouble
```

So, if you happen to define a variable CityTemp like this:

```
FlpCompDouble CityTemp;
```

You will be able to access each of the different parts of the union as follows:

```
CityTemp.d
CityTemp.fd
CityTemp.ul[1] and CityTemp.ul[2]
CityTemp.fdb
```

The two modes that will interest you the most are **.d** and **.fd**. You can make direct assignments to the CityTemp FP variable using **CityTemp.d**, but you can only use Palm's FP function using **CityTemp.fd**.

Palm's FP Functions

The Palm API's **Float Manager** section covers all the floating-point functions you can use with FlpCompDouble variables. I would imagine you will get lots of use out of the **FlpAToF** (convert a string to an FP number) and **FlpFToA** (convert an FP number to a string) functions, since you'll need them for reading input to and from text field controls.

MathLib's FP Functions

MathLib's floating-point functions take over where Palm's end, effectively. Here is a partial list of the functions, many of which you'd find on any good scientific calculator:

- arccosine
- arcsine
- arctangent
- cosine
- sine
- tangent
- hyperbolic cosine
- hyperbolic sine
- hyperbolic tangent
- hyperbolic arccosine
- hyperbolic arcsine
- hyperbolic arctangent
- e^x
- natural logarithm
- base-10 logarithm
- x^y
- square root
- ceiling value
- floor value
- remainder
- round value
- truncate value
- is-infinite (Boolean test function)
- is-finite (Boolean test function)
- is-not-a-number (Boolean test function)

Example Of Invoking A MathLib Function

So that you have a clearer idea of how to use MathLib, here is an example of what you would do. After including MathLib.c in your project, you would need to declare any floating-point variables you would need, such as:

```
FlpCompDouble operand1;
FlpCompDouble operand2;
FlpCompDouble operand3;
```

To assign a value to any FP variable, remember that you're working with a union, and must use the "**.d**" qualifier. So elsewhere in your code, in one of your own functions, you might have statements like the following:

```
operand1.d = 2.56;
operand2.d = 18;
```

Finally, there's the matter of actually coding the function call. If, for example, we want to take the value of operand1 and raise it to the value of operand2 and assign the result to operand3, our statement would need to be:

```
operand3.d = pow(operand1.d, operand2.d);
```

Remember that all the MathLib function names, as with all C function names, are case-sensitive.

If we then wanted to take the resulting operand3 value and use it in one of the Palm API functions for manipulating floating point numbers, we would then use the "**.fd**" qualifier ("fd" for FlpDouble). Remember, since we're using a union we're actually referring to the same physical data memory with multiple names.

Suppose we want to convert the floating-point number to a character string. Assuming we've declared a string variable thus:

```
Char* op3str;
```

We could write the following function call to convert the FP number operand3 to the character string op3str for display in a text field on a Palm form:

```
FplFToA(operand3.fd, op3str);
```

And that, in essence, is how you use MathLib.

16. Coding Tips

In this chapter, I have a collection of tips and hints for coding your Palm project.

The Organized Way To Start A Palm Project

Here is a checklist of steps for starting a new Palm project.

- Gather the source code for any previous Palm projects on which you've worked. Reusing code will save you time and headaches.

- Create a **custom alert** with three blanks (^1 ^2 ^3). You will use this as a debugging aid or if you just want a quick and dirty way to display a message. Add a constant (with a name like **myAlert**) so you can use it easily.

- Create your **Palm forms and controls**. Leave the Resource editor open and click around each of your controls, noting the **control ID** numbers on each. Then define constants at the top of your Palm **AppMain.c** file. This is an easy part of the process and will allow you to feel some progress.

- Create the **event handler code** for any buttons you make, mainly by copying existing event handler code and modifying it, then giving it its own unique name. Run intermediate tests along with way, as you code, using the custom alert to confirm you have the code in the right place for the right button or control. Remember that if your form has more than one button, you'll need a switch statement to check the value of *pEvent->data.ctlSelect.controlID*.

- Create the routines (functions) for any buttons you click and code them in the event handler function.

- Create a routine for opening your PDB database. Place a line calling the routine in your **frmOpenEvent** section. If you can't open the database,

175

use your custom alert to send a message to the user that they need to install the database before using your application, or just create a new database on the fly if that's what you prefer.

- Create a routine for closing the PDB database.

Using Full Screen (No Title Bar)

To get rid of the title line, just set it to a value of null. You'll be able to use the full screen resolution of 160x160 (standard density) or 320x320 (double density). This is especially helpful if you're designing a game and want the full screen for the playfield.

In Strings, A Null Is A Stop Sign

Remember that in operations involving character strings, a value of NULL (or 00 hex) acts like a Stop sign. The Palm function **StrLen** counts the length of a string up to the first null it finds. Also, remember that if you want a character string to be able to hold N characters, you must define it as having length $N+1$. This is especially important when defining typedef record structures. (Example: If you have a program with a LastName value of length 40, your variable should be defined as length 41.)

Use Your Old Projects! Save Your Old Code!

I cannot stress this enough, it will save you loads of time. Once you've successfully written a project, SAVE IT. You can "borrow" routines from yourself or help jog loose a coding technique you were trying to remember. For me, this has been a big time saver.

17. Using The Help Facility

The Garnet OS Development Suite has a very good Help facility. I would recommend you become very familiar with this part of the GDS system.

The Help facility can be found on the menu bar from **Help → Help Contents**, shown in Figure 76.

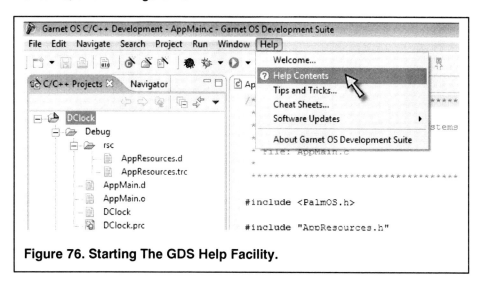

Figure 76. Starting The GDS Help Facility.

Once you click on Help Contents, the GDS Help Facility opens. The home screen is shown in Figure 77 on the next page.

Clicking on **Palm OS 68K API Documentation** opens up what I would argue is the most helpful part of the system – the reference to all the Palm API functions. I would advise you to click around and get familiar with all four parts of the API section – the **Programmer's Companion**, the **API Reference**, and the **User Interface Guidelines**. All this information is also available on ACCESS Company's Palm Developer web site.

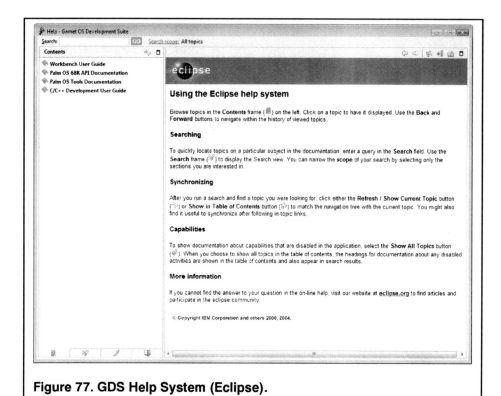

Figure 77. GDS Help System (Eclipse).

The entire Help system can be searched as on a search engine. If, for example, you're looking at someone else's code sample and you see a function you don't recognize – such as **FldScrollField** – you can type the name of that function in the **Search** box. Or even if you have a vague idea of what you're seeking, type that term in the Search box – like "fields", or "memory handles", or "pointers".

The left side of the window shows, in declining order of relevance, links to the information you're seeking. Higher percentages indicate topics more closely related to your search term.

In addition, code samples contained in the Help facility can be copied and pasted into your Palm C project.

And remember this: the Help facility *does not* require an Internet connection to operate – it is its own built-in search engine.

Useful Search Terms

Since you may not exactly be sure what would help you search, I here present a list of terms you can type in the search box. These are terms I have typed myself when looking for something.

For better search results, I suggest opening the **"Palm OS 68K API Documentation"** node of the documentation tree, and then clicking on the **"Palm OS Programmer's API Reference"**. This will bring up the Table of Contents page, as shown in Figure 78. The Search box is circled.

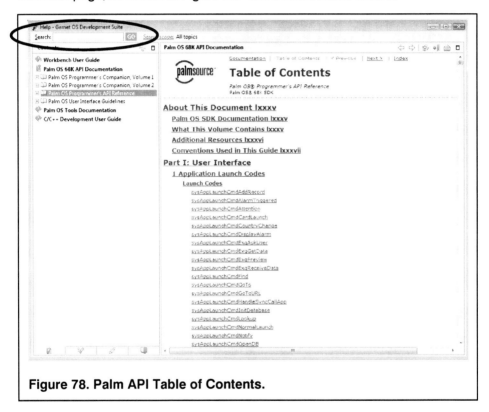

Figure 78. Palm API Table of Contents.

Try searching with any of the following terms:

- **forms**
- **fields**
- **memory manager**
- **strings**

- **bitmaps**
- **dates**
- **time manager**
- **errors**
- **float manager**
- **events**
- **data manager**

Since searches usually bring up more than one possible link in the left window pane, you might need to click several to find the information you're seeking.

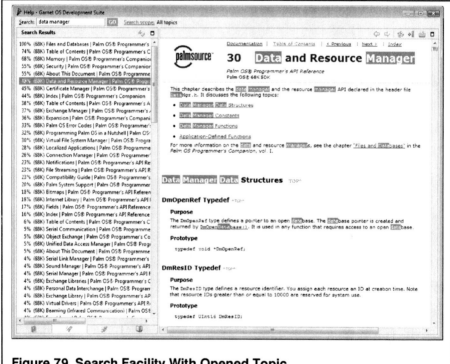

Figure 79. Search Facility With Opened Topic.

Also, note that any terms you typed in the Search box are highlighted so you can find them easily.

Navigation And Control Buttons

As with any web browser, there are navigation buttons in the Help facility to allow you to go back to previous subjects, to bookmark your favorite pages, and to print Help content.

You can discover what each button does by moving your cursor over each.

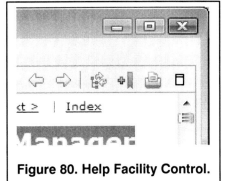

Figure 80. Help Facility Control.

18. A Few Closing Words

Well, if you have read every chapter of this book and tried every exercise and run them successfully, you have acquired a basic proficiency in writing Palm applications, and I have met my goal. But before you close this book, I wanted to add a few final thoughts.

Obviously, this book has not covered everything there is to know about developing Palm applications. It was never my goal for this book to be a comprehensive volume for that purpose. If I had, it would have been at least 500 pages. Besides, there are many other books – two of which I list in the next chapter – that have far more depth and information than I could begin to present here. This book was intended to bridge you from your beginning stages as a Palm developer and to prepare you to reach higher in the Palm universe, should you desire it.

Things You May Want To Pursue On Your Own

So what kinds of things are beyond the scope of this book that you may want to learn for yourself? Here's a partial list:

- More on event handling – including detecting not just where the screen is tapped, but how many times, and whether the stylus is dragged across the screen.

- Reading and writing to external storage devices – some Palm devices have slots for removable storage such as SD cards.

- Reading information from other I/O ports, such as a Bluetooth connection. Perhaps you may write an application that has your Palm device talking to a computer.

- Audio and video – the Palm platform supports sound and video. If you're interested in writing a game with sound, learning about Palm's audio support is a must.

- Larger screen control – devices like the LifeDrive and the T|X feature 320x480 resolution, meaning your application can be smart enough to run in a larger screen. The T|X device also can rotate 90 degrees – how would that affect the design of your application?

The Sky's The Limit

What you create for your Palm device is limited only by your imagination – and, of course, your ability to learn the API function calls and coding techniques to flesh out your algorithms.

Whatever you decide to do, whether it's a small freeware utility or the next great killer app, I'm glad you decided to pick up this book and learn about Palm software development – because if you can envision a Palm application, there's probably some Palm user out there, somewhere, that would enjoy using it.

19. Additional Resources

Looking for more help and support with writing Palm software? I can recommend the following resources, because I've used them myself.

Suggested Reading

Palm Programmer's Bible, Second Edition. Author: Lonnon R. Foster. Publisher: Wiley. Available at Amazon.com.

Palm OS Programming, The Developer's Guide, Second Edition. Authors: Neil Rhodes, Julie McKeehan. Publisher: O'Reilly. Available from the publisher.

On The World Wide Web

ACCESS Developer Network (ADN)
http://www.accessdevnet.com
The ACCESS Developer Network is a resource for Palm developers. Membership is free.

Yahoo! Groups for Palm
http://groups.yahoo.com
In the Search box, type "palm users" or similar search terms.

PocketGear.com
http://www.pocketgear.com
When you're ready to share your creation with the Palm world, whether it's freeware, shareware, or a title you wish to sell, PocketGear.com is a great place to start.

Index

erase text, 126
Err getting rec, 149
eType, 46
event handler, 47, 65, 102, 175
event handling routine, 34
EventType, 70
EvtGetEvent, 44
Existing Project Into Workspace, 96
Extensible Markup Language, 89

F

fatal error, 145, 147
fatal errors, 146
Feedback Slider Control, 98
Field, 61, 98
Field cannot be editable, 149
Field functions, 26
Field is using a handle – setting the
    pointer is invalid, 150
Field object improperly locked, 150
fields, 83, 178
Files, 66, 91, 98, 116
Fireworks, 107
FldDrawField, 26
FldGetTextHandle, 26
FldGetTextPtr, 26
FldRecalculateField, 27
FldScrollField, 178
FldSetTextHandle, 26
FldSetTextPtr, 27, 72, 122
Float Manager, 173
Floating-point, 9
Floating-point numbers, 172
FlpAToF, 173
FlpCompDouble, 9, 172
FlpFToA, 173
Font, 75
for-loop, 13
Form 1000, 61
Form already loaded, 151
Form folder, 60
Form functions, 22
form handler, 49
formId, 46

forms, 60, 175
FP variable, 174
Free handle, 151
FrmCloseAllForms, 45
FrmCustomAlert, 22, 74
FrmDeleteForm, 50
FrmDispatchEvent, 44
FrmDoDialog, 49
FrmDrawForm, 23, 49, 122, 126
FrmGetActiveForm, 22, 48, 122
FrmGetObjectIndex, 22
FrmGetObjectPtr, 22
FrmGotoForm, 23, 45
FrmInitForm, 23, 46, 49
frmLoadEvent, 46
frmOpenEvent, 48, 69, 102, 175
FrmSetActiveForm, 46
FrmSetEventHandler, 47
function, duplicating to debug, 145
functions, 14

G

Garnet, 2
Garnet OS Emulator, 73, 124, 147
Garnet OS Settings window, 97
Garnet OS Simluator, 104
Garnet OS Simulator, 52, 53, 65, 68, 70,
    76, 84, 101
global character string variable, 15
Graffiti, 46, 55
graphic objects, 107

H

handle, 19
handle the actions, 65
handled, 50
handles, 146
Handspring, 3
header files, 42
Hello, World!, 52
Help facility, 70, 177
Help Facility, 121
Help facility, navigation buttons, 181

About The Author

CHARLES TATUM II is a graduate of The University Of Illinois at Urbana-Champaign. He has worked in the field of information technology for over twenty years, including a six-year stint at IBM in Houston. He has served in a variety of roles in the information technology industry including software developer, software tester, web designer, and technical writer. This is his first technical book.

CPSIA information can be obtained at www.ICGtesting.com
Printed in the USA
BVOW03*0740220916

462503BV00018B/18/P